FRACTIONS, DECIMALS, & PERCENTS

GRE Math Preparation Guide

This book provides an in-depth look at the array of GRE questions that test knowledge of Fractions, Decimals, and Percents. Learn to see the connections among these part–whole relationships and practice implementing strategic shortcuts.

Fractions, Decimals, & Percents GRE Strategy Guide, First Edition

10-digit International Standard Book Number: 1-935707-03-5
13-digit International Standard Book Number: 978-1-935707-03-5

8 GUIDE INSTRUCTIONAL SERIES

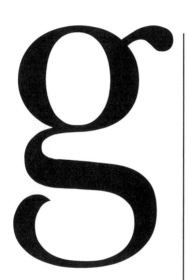

Math GRE Strategy Guides

Algebra
(ISBN: 978-1-935707-02-8)

Fractions, Decimals, & Percents
(ISBN: 978-1-935707-03-5)

Geometry
(ISBN: 978-1-935707-04-2)

Number Properties
(ISBN: 978-1-935707-05-9)

Word Translations
(ISBN: 978-1-935707-06-6)

Quantitative Comparisons & Data Interpretation
(ISBN: 978-1-935707-07-3)

Verbal GRE Strategy Guides

Reading Comprehension & Essays
(ISBN: 978-1-935707-08-0)

ASA: Antonyms, Sentence Completion, Analogies
(ISBN: 978-1-935707-09-7)

Manhattan GRE

September 1st, 2010

Dear Student,

Thank you for picking up one of the Manhattan GRE Strategy Guides—we hope that it refreshes your memory of junior-high school math that you haven't used in years. Maybe it will even teach you a new thing or two.

As with most accomplishments, there were many people involved in the book that you're holding. First and foremost is Zeke Vanderhoek, the founder of MG Prep. Zeke was a lone tutor in New York when he started the Company in 2000. Now, ten years later, the Company has Instructors and offices nationwide and contributes to the studies and successes of thousands of students each year.

Our Manhattan GRE Strategy Guides are based on the continuing experiences of our Instructors and our students. On the Company side, we are indebted to many of our Instructors, including but not limited to Jen Dziura, Stacey Koprince, David Mahler, Chris Ryan, Michael Schwartz, and Tommy Wallach, all of whom either wrote or edited the books to their present form. Dan McNaney and Cathy Huang provided their formatting expertise to make the books as user-friendly as possible. Last, many people, too numerous to list here but no less appreciated, assisted in the development of the online resources that accompany this guide.

At Manhattan GRE, we continually aspire to provide the best Instructors and resources possible. We hope that you'll find our dedication manifest in this book. If you have any comments or questions, please e-mail me at andrew.yang@manhattangre.com. I'll be sure that your comments reach Chris and the rest of the team—and I'll read them too.

Best of luck in preparing for the GRE!

Sincerely,

Andrew Yang
President
Manhattan GRE

HOW TO ACCESS YOUR ONLINE STUDY CENTER

If you…

⊘ **are a registered Manhattan GRE student**

and have received this book as part of your course materials, you have AUTOMATIC access to ALL of our online resources. To access these resources, follow the instructions in the Welcome Guide provided to you at the start of your program. Do NOT follow the instructions below.

⊘ **purchased this book from the Manhattan GRE Online store or at one of our Centers**

1. Go to: http://www.manhattangre.com/studycenter.cfm

2. Log in using the username and password used when your account was set up.

⊘ **purchased this book at a retail location**

1. Go to: http://www.manhattangre.com/access.cfm

2. Log in or create an account.

3. Follow the instructions on the screen.

Your one year of online access begins on the day that you register your book at the above URL.

You only need to register your product ONCE at the above URL. To use your online resources any time AFTER you have completed the registration process, login to the following URL: http://www.manhattangre.com/studycenter.cfm

Please note that online access is non-transferable. This means that only NEW and UNREGISTERED copies of the book will grant you online access. Previously used books will not provide any online resources.

⊘ **purchased an e-book version of this book**

Email a copy of your purchase receipt to books@manhattangre.com to activate your resources.

For any technical issues, email books@manhattangre.com or call 800-576-4628.

Introduction, and How to Use Manhattan GRE's Strategy Guides

We know that you're looking to succeed on the GRE so that you can go to graduate school and do the things you want to do in life.

We also know that you might not have done math since high school, and that you may never have learned words like "adumbrate" or "sangfroid." We know that it's going to take hard work on your part to get a top GRE score, and that's why we've put together the only set of books that will take you from the basics all the way up to the material you need to master for a near-perfect score, or whatever your score goal may be.

How a Computer Adaptive Test Works

On paper-based tests, top scores are achieved by solving a mix of easy and medium questions, with a few hard ones at the end. The GRE is totally different.

The GRE is a computer adaptive test (or "CAT"). That means that the better you do, the harder the material you will see (and the worse you do, the easier the material you will see). Your ultimate score isn't based on how many questions you got right—it's based on "testing into" a high level of difficulty, and then performing well enough to stay at that difficulty level. In other words, you *want* to see mostly hard questions.

This book was written by a team of test prep professionals, including instructors who have scored perfect 1600s repeatedly on the GRE, and who have taught and tutored literally thousands of students at all levels of performance. We don't just focus on "tricks"—on a test that adapts to your performance, it's important to know the real material being tested.

Speed and Pacing

Most people can sum up the numbers from 1–20, if they have enough time. Most people can also tell you whether 789×791 is bigger than 788×792, if they have enough time. Few people can do these things in the 1–2 minutes per problem allotted on the GRE.

If you've taken a practice test (visit **www.manhattangre.com** for information about this), you may have had serious trouble finishing the test before time ran out. On the GRE, it is extremely important that you finish every question. (You also may not skip questions or return to any previously answered question). In these books, you'll find ways to do things fast—very fast.

As a reference, here's about how much time you should spend on each problem type on the GRE:

Analogies – **45 seconds**
Sentence Correction – **1 minute**
Problem Solving and Data Interpretation – **2 minutes**

Antonyms – **30 seconds**
Reading Comprehension – **1.5 minutes**
Quantitative Comparison – **1 min 15 seconds**

Of course, no one can time each question this precisely while taking the actual test—instead, you will see a timer on the screen that counts down (from 30 minutes on Verbal, and from 45 minutes on Quant), and you must keep an eye on that clock and manage time as you go. Manhattan GRE's strategies will help you solve questions extremely efficiently.

How to Use These Materials

Manhattan GRE's materials are comprehensive. But keep in mind that, depending on your score goal, it may not be necessary to "get" absolutely everything. Grad schools only see your overall Quantitative, Verbal, and Writing scores—they don't see exactly which strengths and weaknesses went into creating those scores.

You may be enrolled in one of our courses, in which case you already have a syllabus telling you in what order you should approach the books. But if you bought this book online or at a bookstore, feel free to approach the books—and even the chapters within the books—in whatever order works best for you. *For the most part, the books, and the chapters within them, are independent; you don't have to master one section before moving on to the next.* So if you're having a hard time with something in particular, you can make a note to come back to it later and move on to another section. Similarly, it may not be necessary to solve every single practice problem for every section. As you go through the material, continually assess whether you understand and can apply the principles in each individual section and chapter. The best way to do this is to solve the Check Your Skills and Practice Problems throughout. If you're confident you have a concept or method down, feel free to move on. If you struggle with something, make note of it for further review. Stay active in your learning and oriented toward the test—it's easy to read something and think you understand it, only to have trouble applying it in the 1–2 minutes you have to solve a problem.

Study Skills

As you're studying for the GRE, try to integrate your learning into your everyday life. For example, vocabulary is a big part of the GRE, as well as something you just can't "cram" for—you're going to want to do at least a little bit of vocab every day. So, try to learn and internalize a little bit at a time, switching up topics often to help keep things interesting.

Keep in mind that, while many of your study materials are on paper (including ETS's most recent source of official GRE questions, *Practicing to Take the GRE General Test 10th Edition*), your exam will be administered on a computer. The testing center will provide you with pencils and a booklet of bound, light-blue paper. If you run out, you may request a new booklet, but you may only have one at a time. Because this is a computer-based test, you will NOT be able to underline portions of reading passages, write on diagrams of geometry figures, or otherwise physically mark up problems. So get used to this now. Solve the problems in these books on scratch paper. (Each of our books talks specifically about what to write down for different problem types).

Again, as you study stay focused on the test-day experience. As you progress, work on timed drills and sets of questions. Eventually, you should be taking full practice tests (available at www.manhattangre.com) under realistic timed conditions.

Changes to the Exam

Finally, you've probably heard that the GRE is changing in August, 2011. Look in the back of this book for more information about the switch—every one of these GRE books contains additional material for the 2011 GRE, and we'll be constantly updating **www.manhattangre.com** as new information becomes available. If you're going to take the test before the changeover, it's nothing to worry about.

Diving In

While we love standardized tests, we understand that your goal is really about grad school, and your life beyond that. However, you'll make your way through these books much more easily—and much more pleasantly—if you can stay positive and engaged throughout. Hopefully, the process of studying for the GRE will make your brain a more interesting place to be! Now let's get started!

TABLE OF CONTENTS

g

Chapter 1
of
FRACTIONS, DECIMALS, & PERCENTS

FRACTIONS

In This Chapter . . .

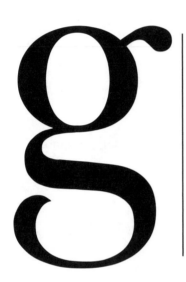

- Manipulating Fractions
- Switching Between Improper Fractions and Mixed Numbers
- Division in Disguise
- Fraction Operations: Funky Results
- Comparing Fractions: Cross-Multiply
- Never Split the Denominator
- Benchmark Values
- Smart Numbers: Multiples of the Denominator
- When Not to Use Smart Numbers

FRACTIONS

This chapter is devoted entirely to understanding what fractions are and how they work from the ground up. Let's begin by reviewing the two parts of a fraction: the **numerator** and the **denominator.**

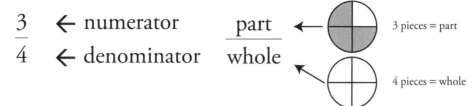

In the picture above, each circle represents a whole unit. One full circle means the number 1, 2 full circles is 2, etc. Fractions essentially divide units into parts. The units above have been divided into 4 equal parts, because the denominator of our fraction is 4. In any fraction, the denominator tells you how many equal pieces a unit has been broken into.

The circle at the top has 3 of the pieces shaded in, and one piece unshaded. That's because the top of our fraction is 3. For any fraction, the numerator tells you how many of the equal pieces you have.

Let's see how changes to the numerator and denominator change a fraction. We'll start by seeing how changes affect the denominator. You've already seen what 3/4 looks like; let's see what 3/5 looks like.

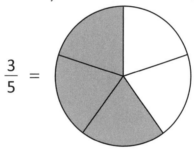

The numerator hasn't changed (it's still 3), so we still have 3 shaded pieces. But now the circle has been divided into 5 pieces instead of 4. One effect is that each piece is now smaller. 1/5 is smaller than 1/4. In general, as the denominator of a number gets bigger, the value of the fraction gets smaller. 3/5 is smaller than 3/4, because each fraction has 3 pieces, but when the circle (or number) is divided into 5 equal portions, each portion is smaller, so 3 portions of 1/5 are less than 3 portions of 1/4.

As we split the circle into more and more pieces, each piece gets smaller and smaller. Conversely, as the denominator gets smaller, each piece becomes bigger and bigger.

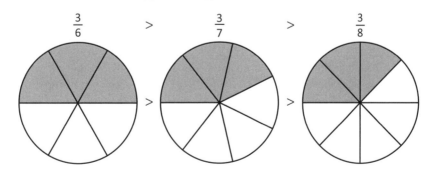

Now let's see what happens as we change the numerator. The numerator tells us how many pieces we have, so if we make the numerator smaller, we get fewer pieces.

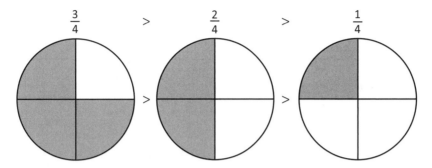

Conversely, if we make the numerator larger, we get more pieces. Let's look more closely what happens as we get more pieces. In particular, we want to know what happens when the numerator becomes equal to or greater than the denominator. First, let's see what happens when we have the same numerator and denominator. If we have 4/4 pieces, this is what our circle looks like.

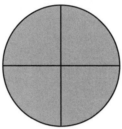

Remember, our circle represents one whole unit. So when all four parts are filled, we have one full unit, or 1. So 4/4 is equal to 1. In general, if the numerator and denominator of a fraction are the same, that fraction equals 1.

Now let's see what happens as the numerator becomes larger than the denominator. What does 5/4 look like?

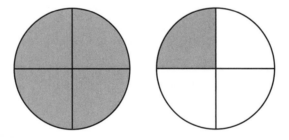

Each circle is only capable of holding 4 pieces, so when we fill up one circle, we have to move on to a second circle and begin filling it up too. So one way of looking at 5/4 is that we have one complete circle, which we know is equivalent to 1, and we have an additional 1/4. So another way to write 5/4 is 1 + 1/4. This can be shortened to $1\frac{1}{4}$ ("one and one fourth").

In the last example, the numerator was only a little larger than the denominator. But that will not always be the case. The same logic applies to any situation. Look at the fraction 15/4. Once again, this means that each number is divided into 4 pieces, and we have 15 pieces.

$$\frac{15}{4} =$$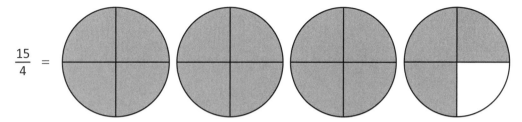

In this case, we have 3 circles completely filled. To fill 3 circles, we needed 12 pieces. (Note: 3 circles × 4 pieces per circle = 12 pieces.) In addition to the 3 full circles, we have 3 additional pieces. So we have $\frac{15}{4} = 3 + \frac{3}{4} = 3\frac{3}{4}$.

Whenever you have both an integer and a fraction in the same number, you have a **mixed number.** Meanwhile, any fraction in which the numerator is larger than the denominator (for example, 5/4) is known as an **improper fraction.** Improper fractions and mixed numbers express the same thing. Later in the chapter we'll discuss how to change from improper fractions to mixed numbers and vice-versa.

Let's review what we've learned about fractions so far. Every fraction has two components: the numerator and the denominator.

The denominator tells you how many equal pieces each unit circle has. As the denominator gets bigger, each piece gets smaller, so the fraction gets smaller as well.

The numerator tells you how many equal pieces you have. As the numerator gets bigger, you have more pieces, so the fraction gets bigger.

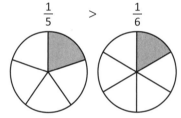

When the numerator is smaller than the denominator, the fraction will be less than 1. When the numerator equals the denominator, the fraction equals 1. When the numerator is larger than the denominator, the fraction is greater than 1.

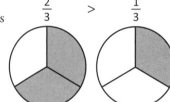

Check Your Skills
For each of the following sets of fractions, decide which fraction is larger.

1. $\frac{5}{7}, \frac{3}{7}$

2. $\frac{3}{10}, \frac{3}{13}$

Answers can be found on page 41.

Manipulating Fractions

In the next two sections, we'll discuss how to add, subtract, multiply and divide fractions. We're already familiar with these four basic manipulations of arithmetic, but when fractions enter the picture, things can become more complicated.

Below, we're going to discuss each manipulation in turn. In each discussion, we'll first talk conceptually about what changes are being made with each manipulation. Then we'll go through the actual mechanics of performing the manipulation.

We'll begin with how to add and subtract fractions.

Fraction Addition and Subtraction

The first thing to recall about addition and subtraction in general is that they affect how many things you have. If you have 3 things, and you add 6 more things, you have 3 + 6 = 9 things. If you have 7 things and you subtract, or take away, 2 of those things, you now have 7 − 2 = 5 things. That same basic principle holds true with fractions as well. What this means is that addition and subtraction affect the numerator of a fraction, because the numerator tells us how many things, or pieces, we have.

For example, let's say we want to add the two fractions 1/5 and 3/5. What we are doing is adding 3 fifths to 1 fifth. (A "fifth" is the very specific pie slice we see below.)

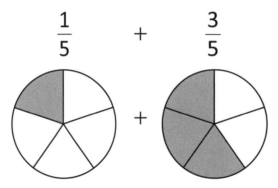

If we were dealing with integers, and we added 3 to 1, we would get 4. The idea is the same with fractions. Now, instead of adding 3 complete units to one complete unit, we're adding 3 fifths to 1 fifth. 1 fifth plus 3 fifths equals 4 fifths.

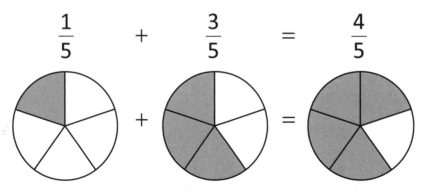

Notice that when we added the two fractions, the denominator stayed the same. Remember, the denominator tells you how many pieces each unit circle has been broken into. In other words, it determines the size of the slice. Adding 3 pieces to 1 piece did nothing to change the size of the pieces. Each unit is still broken into 5 pieces; hence there is no change to the denominator. The only effect of the addition was to end up with more pieces, which means that we ended up with a larger numerator.

Be able to conceptualize what we just did both ways: adding 1/5 and 3/5 to get 4/5, *and* regarding 4/5 as the sum of 1/5 and 3/5.

$$\frac{1}{5}+\frac{3}{5}=\frac{1+3}{5}=\frac{4}{5}$$

$$\frac{4}{5}=\frac{1+3}{5}=\frac{1}{5}+\frac{3}{5}$$

Also, you should be able to handle an *x* in place of one of the numerators.

$$\frac{1}{5}+\frac{x}{5}=\frac{4}{5} \text{ becomes } 1+x=4$$
$$x=3$$

We can apply the same thinking no matter what the denominator is. Say we want to add 3/6 and 5/6. This is how it looks.

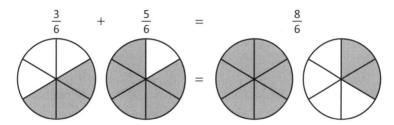

Notice that once again, the only thing that changes during the operation is the numerator. Adding 5 sixths to 3 sixths gives you 8 sixths. The principle is still the same even though we ended up with an improper fraction.

Again, see the operation both ways:

$$\frac{3}{6}+\frac{5}{6}=\frac{3+5}{6}=\frac{8}{6} \qquad \frac{8}{6}=\frac{3+5}{6}=\frac{3}{6}+\frac{5}{6}$$

Be ready for the *x* as well:

$$\frac{3}{6}+\frac{x}{6}=\frac{8}{6} \text{ becomes } 3+x=8$$
$$x=5$$

Now let's look at a slightly different problem. This time we want to add 1/4 and 3/8.

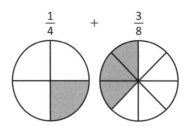

Do you see the problem here? We have one thing on the left and three things on the right, but the denominators are different, so the sizes of the pieces are different. It doesn't make sense in this case simply to add the numerators and get 4 of anything. Fraction addition only works if we can add pieces that are all the same size. So now the question becomes, how can we make all the pieces the same size?

What we need to do is find a new way to express one or both of the fractions so that the slices are the same size. For this particular addition problem, we can take advantage of the fact that one fourth is twice as big as one eighth. Look what happens if we take all the fourths in our first circle and divide them in two.

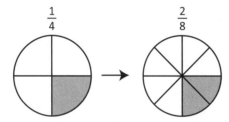

What happened to our fraction? The first thing to note is that we haven't changed the value of our fraction. Originally, we had 1 piece out of 4. Once we divided every part into 2, we ended up with 2 pieces out of 8. So we ended up with twice as many pieces, but each piece was half as big. So we actually ended up with the same amount of stuff overall.

What did we change? We ended up with twice as many pieces, which means we multiplied the numerator by 2, and we broke the circle into twice as many pieces, which means we also multiplied the denominator by 2. So we ended up with $\frac{1 \times 2}{4 \times 2} = \frac{2}{8}$. We'll come back to this concept later, but for now, simply make sure that you understand that $\frac{1}{4} = \frac{2}{8}$.

So without changing the value of 1/4, we've now found a way to *rename* 1/4 as 2/8, so we can add it to 3/8. Now our problem looks like this:

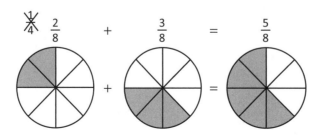

The key to this addition problem was to find what we call a **common denominator.** Finding a common denominator simply means renaming the fractions so they have the same denominator. Then we can add the renamed fractions.

We won't get into all the details of fraction multiplication just yet (don't worry—it's coming), but we need to take a closer look at what we did to the fraction $\frac{1}{4}$ in order to rename it. Essentially what we did was multiply this fraction by $\frac{2}{2}$. $\frac{1}{4} = \frac{1}{4} \times \frac{2}{2} = \frac{1 \times 2}{4 \times 2} = \frac{2}{8}$. As we've already discussed, any fraction in which the numerator equals the denominator is 1. So 2/2 = 1. That means that all we did was multiply 1/4 by 1. And anything times 1 equals itself. So we changed the appearance of 1/4 by multiplying the top and bottom by 2, but we did not change its value.

Finding common denominators is a critical skill when dealing with fractions. Let's walk through another example and see how the process works. This time we're going to add 1/4 and 1/3.

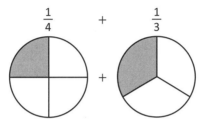

Once again we are adding two fractions with different-sized pieces. There's no way to complete the addition without finding a common denominator. But remember, the only way that we can find common denominators is by multiplying one or both of the fractions by some version of 1 (such as 2/2, 3/3, 4/4, etc.). Because we can only multiply by 1 (the number that won't change the value of the fraction), the only way we can change the denominators is through multiplication. In the last example, the two denominators were 4 and 8. We were able to make them equal because 4 × 2 = 8.

Because all we can do is multiply, what we really need when we look for a common denominator is a common *multiple* of both denominators. In the last example, 8 was a multiple of both 4 and 8.

In this problem, we are adding 1/4 and 1/3. We need to find a number that is a multiple of both 4 and 3. List a few multiples of 4: 4, 8, 12, 16…. Also list a few multiples of 3: 3, 6, 9, 12, stop. 12 is on both lists, so 12 is a multiple of both 3 and 4. Now we need to change both fractions so that they have a denominator of 12.

Let's begin by changing 1/4. We have to ask the question, what times 4 equals 12? The answer is 3. That means that we want to multiply 1/4 by 3/3. $\frac{1}{4} \times \frac{3}{3} = \frac{3}{12}$. So 1/4 is the same as 3/12. Once again, we can look at our circles to verify these fractions are the same.

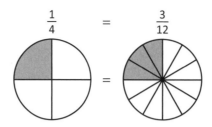

Now we need to change 1/3. Once again, we need to ask, what times 3 equals 12? $4 \times 3 = 12$, so we need to multiply 1/3 by 4/4. $\dfrac{1}{3} = \dfrac{1}{3} \times \dfrac{4}{4} = \dfrac{4}{12}$. Now both of our fractions have a common denominator, so we're ready to add.

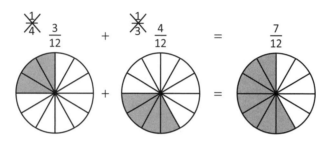

$$\frac{1}{4} + \frac{1}{3} = \frac{1 \times 3}{4 \times 3} + \frac{1 \times 4}{3 \times 4} = \frac{3}{12} + \frac{4}{12} = \frac{7}{12}$$

And now you know everything you need to add any two fractions together.

Let's recap what we've done so far.

When adding fractions, we have to add equal-sized pieces. That means we need the denominators to be the same for any fractions we want to add. **If the denominators are the same, then you add the numerators and keep the denominator the same.**

Ex. $\dfrac{2}{9} + \dfrac{5}{9} = \dfrac{7}{9}$

If the two fractions have different denominators, you need to find a common multiple for the two denominators first.

Ex. $\dfrac{1}{4} + \dfrac{2}{5} = ?$

Common multiple of 4 and 5 = 20

Once you know the common multiple, you need to figure out for each fraction what number times the denominator equals the common multiple.

$\dfrac{1}{4} \times \dfrac{5}{5} = \dfrac{5}{20}$ $\dfrac{2}{5} \times \dfrac{4}{4} = \dfrac{8}{20}$

Using the number you found in the last step, multiply each fraction that needs to be changed by the appropriate fractional version of 1 (such as 5/5).

Now that the denominators are the same, you can add the fractions.

$\dfrac{5}{20} + \dfrac{8}{20} = \dfrac{13}{20}$

This section would not be complete without a discussion of subtraction. The good news is that subtraction works exactly the same way as addition! The only difference is that when you subtract, you end up with fewer pieces instead of more pieces, so you end up with a smaller numerator.

Let's walk through a subtraction problem together. What is 5/7 − 1/3?

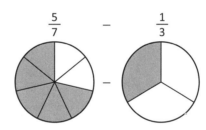

Just like addition, subtraction of fractions requires a common denominator. So we need to figure out a common multiple of the two denominators: 7 and 3. 21 is a common multiple, so let's use that.

Let's change 5/7 so that its denominator is 21. 3 times 7 equals 21, so let's multiply 5/7 by 3/3.
$\dfrac{5}{7} = \dfrac{5}{7} \times \dfrac{3}{3} = \dfrac{15}{21}$. Now we do the same for 1/3. 7 times 3 equals 21, so let's multiply 1/3 by 7/7.
$\dfrac{1}{3} = \dfrac{1}{3} \times \dfrac{7}{7} = \dfrac{7}{21}$. Our subtraction problem can be rewritten as $\dfrac{15}{21} - \dfrac{7}{21}$, which we can easily solve.

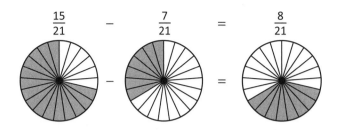

$$\frac{15}{21} - \frac{7}{21} = \frac{8}{21}$$

Finally, if you have an *x* in the addition, nothing really changes. One way or another, you still have to find a common denominator.

Let's try another problem.

Solve: $\dfrac{1}{4} + \dfrac{x}{5} = \dfrac{13}{20}$

First, subtract 1/4 from each side:

$$\frac{x}{5} = \frac{13}{20} - \frac{1}{4}$$

Perform the subtraction by finding the common denominator, which is 20.

$$\frac{13}{20} - \frac{1 \times 5}{4 \times 5} = \frac{13}{20} - \frac{5}{20} = \frac{8}{20}$$

So we have $\dfrac{x}{5} = \dfrac{8}{20}$

There are several options at this point. The one we'll use right now is to convert to the common denominator again (which is still 20).

$$\frac{x \times 4}{5 \times 4} = \frac{4x}{20} = \frac{8}{20}$$

Now we can set the numerators equal: $4x = 8$

Divide by 4: $x = 2$

If we had spotted the common denominator of all 3 fractions at the start, we could have saved work:

$$\frac{1}{4} + \frac{x}{5} = \frac{13}{20}$$

Convert to a common denominator of 20:

$$\frac{1 \times 5}{4 \times 5} + \frac{x \times 4}{5 \times 4} = \frac{13}{20}$$

Clean up:

$$\frac{5}{20} + \frac{4x}{20} = \frac{13}{20}$$

Set numerators equal:

$$5 + 4x = 13$$

Subtract 5:	$4x = 8$
Divide by 4:	$x = 2$

Check Your Skills
Evaluate the following expressions.

3. $\dfrac{1}{2} + \dfrac{3}{4} =$

4. $\dfrac{2}{3} - \dfrac{3}{8} =$

5. Find x. $\dfrac{x}{5} + \dfrac{2}{5} = \dfrac{13}{5}$

6. Find x. $\dfrac{x}{3} - \dfrac{4}{9} = \dfrac{8}{9}$

Answers can be found on page 41.

Simplifying Fractions

Suppose you were presented with this question on the GRE.

$$\frac{5}{9} + \frac{1}{9} = ?$$

a. 4/9   b. 5/9   c. 2/3

This question involves fraction addition, which we know how to do. So let's begin by adding the two fractions. $\dfrac{5}{9} + \dfrac{1}{9} = \dfrac{5+1}{9} = \dfrac{6}{9}$. But 6/9 isn't one of the answer choices. Did we do something wrong? No, we didn't, but we did forget an important step.

6/9 doesn't appear as an answer choice because it isn't **simplified** (or reduced). To understand what that means, we're going to return to a topic that should be very familiar to you at this point—prime factors. Let's break down the numerator and denominator into prime factors. $\dfrac{6}{9} \rightarrow \dfrac{2 \times 3}{3 \times 3}$.

Notice how both the numerator and the denominator have a 3 as one of their prime factors. Because neither multiplying nor dividing by 1 changes the value of a number, we can effectively cancel the $\dfrac{3}{3}$, leaving behind only $\dfrac{2}{3}$. That is, $\dfrac{6}{9} = \dfrac{2 \times \cancel{3}}{3 \times \cancel{3}} = \dfrac{2}{3}$.

Let's look at another example of a fraction that can be reduced: $\dfrac{18}{60}$. Once again, we can begin by breaking the numerator and denominator into their prime factors. $\dfrac{18}{60} \rightarrow \dfrac{2 \times 3 \times 3}{2 \times 2 \times 3 \times 5}$. This time, the numerator and the denominator have two factors in common: a 2 and a 3. Once again, we can split this fraction into two pieces.

$$\frac{2 \times 3 \times 3}{2 \times 2 \times 3 \times 5} \rightarrow \frac{3}{2 \times 5} \times \frac{2 \times 3}{2 \times 3} \rightarrow \frac{3}{10} \times \frac{6}{6}.$$ Once again, $\frac{6}{6}$ is the same as 1, so really we have $\frac{3}{10} \times 1$, which leaves us with $\frac{3}{10}$.

As you practice, you should be able to simplify fractions by recognizing the largest common factor in the numerator and denominator and canceling it out. For example, you should recognize that in the fraction $\frac{18}{60}$, both the numerator and the denominator are divisible by 6. That means we could think of it as $\frac{3 \times 6}{10 \times 6}$. You can then cancel out the common factors on top and bottom and simplify the fraction.

$$\frac{18}{60} = \frac{3 \times \cancel{6}}{10 \times \cancel{6}} = \frac{3}{10}.$$

Check Your Skills
Simplify the following fractions.

7. $\dfrac{25}{40}$

8. $\dfrac{16}{24}$

Answers can be found on page 41.

Fraction Multiplication

Now that we know how to add and subtract fractions, we're ready to multiply and divide them. We'll begin with multiplication. First, we'll talk about what happens when we multiply a fraction by an integer.

We'll start by asking the question, what is 1/2 × 6? When we added and subtracted fractions, we were really adding and subtracting pieces of numbers. With multiplication, we are starting with an amount, and leaving a fraction of it behind. For instance, in this example, what we are really asking is, what is 1/2 *of* 6? There are a few ways to visualize what that means.

We want to find one half of six. One way to do that is to split 6 into 2 equal parts and keep one of those parts.

Because the denominator of our fraction is 2, we divide 6 into 2 equal parts of 3. Then, because our denominator is 1, we keep one of those parts. So 1/2 × 6 = 3.

We can also think of this multiplication problem a slightly different way. Consider each unit circle of the 6. What happens if we break each of those circles into 2 parts, and keep 1 part?

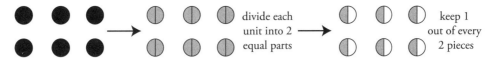

We divide every circle into 2 parts, and keep 1 of every 2 parts. We end up with 6 halves, or 6/2, written as a fraction. But 6/2 is the same as 3, so really, 1/2 of 6 is 3.

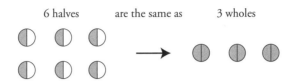

Either way we approach this question, we end up with the same answer. Let's try another example.

What is 2/3 × 12?

Once again, we are really asking, what is 2/3 of 12? In the previous example, when we multiplied a number by 1/2, we divided the number into 2 parts (as indicated by the denominator). Then we kept 1 of those parts (as indicated by the numerator).

By the same logic, if we want to get 2/3 of 12, we need to divide 12 into 3 equal parts, because the denominator is 3. Then we keep 2 of those parts, because the numerator is 2. As with the first example, there are several ways of visualizing this. One way is to divide 12 into 3 equal parts, and keep 2 of those parts.

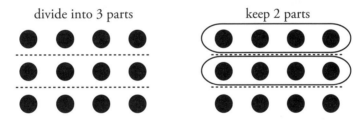

We divided 12 into 3 equal parts of 4, and kept 2 of those parts. 2 groups of 4 is 8, so 2/3 × 12 = 8.

Another way to visualize 2/3 × 12 is to once again look at each unit of 12. If we break each unit into 3 pieces (because the denominator of our fraction is 3) and keep 2 out of every 3 pieces (because our numerator is 2) we end up with this:

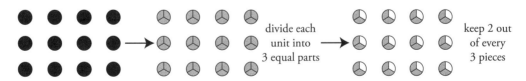

We ended up with 24 thirds, or 24/3. But 24/3 is the same as 8, so 2/3 of 12 is 8.

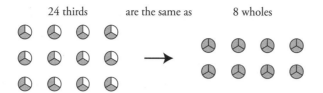

Once again, either way we look at this multiplication problem, we arrive at the same conclusion. 2/3 × 12 = 8.

Now that we've seen what happens when we multiply an integer by a fraction, it's time to multiply a fraction by a fraction. It's important to remember that the basic logic is the same. When you multiply any number by a fraction, the denominator of the fraction tells you how many parts to divide your number into, and the numerator tells you how many of those parts to keep. Now let's see how that logic applies to fractions.

What is 1/2 of 3/4?

This question is asking, what is 1/2 of 3/4? So once again, we need to divide 3/4 into 2 equal parts. This time, though, because we're splitting a fraction, we're going to do things a little differently. Because 3/4 is a fraction, it has already broken a number into 4 equal pieces. So what we're going to do is we're going to break each of those pieces into 2 smaller pieces.

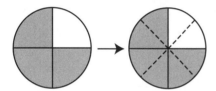

Cut each piece in half

Now that we've divided each piece into 2 smaller pieces, we want to keep 1 of those smaller pieces.

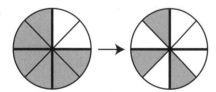

Keep 1 out of 2 resulting pieces.

So what did we end up with? First of all, our product is going to remain a fraction. Our original number was 3/4. In other words, a number was broken into 4 parts, and we had 3 of those parts. Now the number has been broken into 8 pieces, not 4, so our denominator is now 8. However, we still have 3 of those parts, so our numerator is still 3. So 1/2 of 3/4 is 3/8.

Let's try one more. What is 5/6 of 1/2? Once again, we have to start by dividing our fraction into 6 equal pieces.

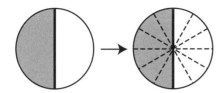

Cut each piece into 6 smaller pieces

Now we want to keep 5 out of every 6 parts.

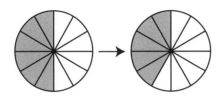

Keep 5 of the 6

So what did we end up with? Now we have a number divided into 12 parts, so our denominator is 12, and we have 5 parts, so the numerator is 5. 5/6 of 1/2 is 5/12.

Now, multiplying fractions would get very cumbersome if we always resorted to slicing circles up into increasingly tiny pieces. So let's talk about the mechanics of multiplying a number by a fraction.

First, note the following crucial difference between two types of arithmetic operations:

Addition & Subtraction:
Only the numerator changes (once you've found a common denominator).

Multiplication & Division:
Both numerator and denominator typically change.

Now, to multiply fractions, you just multiply together the numerators to get the new numerator. You multiply the denominators together to get the new denominator. Then you simplify.

$$\frac{1}{2} \times \frac{6}{1} = \frac{1 \times 6}{2 \times 1} = \frac{6}{2} = 3$$

$$\frac{2}{3} \times \frac{12}{1} = \frac{2 \times 12}{3 \times 1} = \frac{24}{3} = 8$$

$$\frac{1}{2} \times \frac{3}{4} = \frac{1 \times 3}{2 \times 4} = \frac{3}{8}$$

$$\frac{5}{6} \times \frac{1}{2} = \frac{5 \times 1}{6 \times 2} = \frac{5}{12}$$

In practice, when you are multiplying fractions, don't worry about the conceptual foundation, which is much harder to grasp than the mechanics.

Mechanics: $\dfrac{1}{2} \times \dfrac{3}{4} = \dfrac{1 \times 3}{2 \times 4} = \dfrac{3}{8}$ EASIER

$\dfrac{1}{2} \times \dfrac{3}{4}$

Conceptual: "one half of 3/8"…cut up the circles further… HARDER

Lastly, whenever we multiply fractions, we should always look to cancel common factors, in order to reduce our answer without doing unnecessary work.

$$\dfrac{33}{7} \times \dfrac{14}{3} = ?$$

Long way: $33 \times 14 =$

$$\begin{array}{r} {}^{1}33 \\ \times\ 14 \\ \hline 132 \\ 330 \\ \hline 462 \end{array}$$

$7 \times 3 = 21$

You wind up with $\dfrac{462}{21}$.

$$\begin{array}{r} 22 \\ 21\overline{)462} \\ -42 \\ \hline 42 \\ -42 \\ \hline \end{array}$$

This work can be simplified greatly by canceling parts of each fraction before multiplying. Shortcut: Look for common factors in the numerator and denominator.

$$\dfrac{33}{7} \times \dfrac{14}{3} = \dfrac{3 \times 11}{7} \times \dfrac{2 \times 7}{3}$$

We can now see that the numerator of the first fraction has a 3 as a factor, which can be canceled out by the 3 in the denominator of the second fraction. Similarly, the 7 in the denominator of the first fraction can be canceled out by the 7 in the numerator of the second fraction. By cross-canceling these factors, we can save ourselves a lot of work.

$$\dfrac{\cancel{3} \times 11}{\cancel{7}} \times \dfrac{2 \times \cancel{7}}{\cancel{3}} = \dfrac{11}{1} \times \dfrac{2}{1} = \dfrac{22}{1} = 22$$

Check Your Skills

Evaluate the following expressions. Simplify all fractions.

9. $\dfrac{3}{7} \times \dfrac{6}{10} =$

10. $\dfrac{5}{14} \times \dfrac{7}{20} =$

Answers can be found on page 41.

Fraction Division

Now we're up to the last of our four basic operations (addition, subtraction, multiplication and division). This section will be a little different than the other three. The reason it will be different is that we're actually going to do fraction division by avoiding division altogether!

We can avoid division entirely because of the relationship between multiplication and division. Multiplication and division are two sides of the same coin. Any multiplication problem can be expressed as a division problem, and vice-versa. This is useful because, although the mechanics for multiplication are straightforward, the mechanics for division are complicated. Because division is more difficult to perform than multiplication, we are going to express every fraction division problem as a fraction multiplication problem.

Now the question becomes, how do we rephrase a division problem so that it becomes a multiplication problem? The key is **reciprocals.**

Reciprocals are numbers that, when multiplied together, equal 1. For instance, 3/5 and 5/3 are reciprocals, because $\dfrac{3}{5} \times \dfrac{5}{3} = \dfrac{3 \times 5}{5 \times 3} = \dfrac{15}{15} = 1$.

Another pair of reciprocals is 2 and 1/2, because $2 \times \dfrac{1}{2} = \dfrac{2}{1} \times \dfrac{1}{2} = \dfrac{2 \times 1}{1 \times 2} = \dfrac{2}{2} = 1$. Once again, it is important to remember that every integer can be thought of as a fraction.

The way to find the reciprocal of a number turns out to be very easy—take the numerator and denominator of a number and switch them.

Reciprocals are important because dividing by a number is the exact same thing as multiplying by its reciprocal. Let's look at an example to clarify.

What is 6 ÷ 2?

This problem shouldn't give you any trouble—6 divided by 2 is 3. But it should also seem familiar. In reality, it's the exact same problem we dealt with in the discussion on fraction multiplication. 6 ÷ 2 is the exact same thing as 6 × 1/2.

$6 \div 2 = 3$
$6 \times 1/2 = 3$ Dividing by 2 is the same as multiplying by 1/2.

To change from division to multiplication, you need to do two things. First, take the divisor (the number to the right of the division sign—in other words, what you are dividing *by*) and replace it with its reciprocal. In this problem, 2 is the divisor, and 1/2 is the reciprocal of 2. Then, switch the division sign to a multiplication sign. So 6 ÷ 2 becomes 6 × 1/2. Then, proceed to do the multiplication.

$$6 \div 2 = 6 \times \frac{1}{2} = \frac{6}{1} \times \frac{1}{2} = \frac{6 \times 1}{1 \times 2} = \frac{6}{2} = 3.$$

This is obviously overkill for 6 ÷ 2, but let's try another one. What is 5/6 ÷ 4/7?

Once again, we start by taking the divisor (4/7) and replacing it with its reciprocal (7/4). We then switch the division sign to a multiplication sign. So 5/6 ÷ 4/7 is the same as 5/6 × 7/4. Now we do fraction multiplication. $\frac{5}{6} \div \frac{4}{7} = \frac{5}{6} \times \frac{7}{4} = \frac{5 \times 7}{6 \times 4} = \frac{35}{24}$. And that's all there is to it.

Note that the fraction bar or slash is another way to express division. After all, $6 \div 2 = 6/2 = \frac{6}{2} = 3$. In fact, the division sign ÷ looks like a little fraction. So if you see a "double-decker" fraction, don't worry. It's just one fraction divided by another fraction.

$$\frac{\frac{5}{6}}{\frac{4}{7}} = \frac{5}{6} \div \frac{4}{7} = \frac{5}{6} \times \frac{7}{4} = \frac{35}{24}$$

Let's recap. When you are confronted with a division problem involving fractions, it is *always* easier to perform multiplication than division. For that reason, every division problem should be rewritten as a multiplication problem.

To do so, replace the divisor with its reciprocal. To find the reciprocal of a number, you simply need to switch the numerator and denominator (ex. 2/9 → 9/2).

Remember that a number multiplied by its reciprocal equals 1.

After that, switch the division symbol to a multiplication symbol, and perform fraction multiplication.

Fraction	Reciprocal
$\frac{2}{9}$ →	$\frac{9}{2}$

$$\frac{9}{2} \times \frac{2}{9} = 1$$

$$\frac{3}{4} \div \frac{2}{9} \rightarrow \frac{3}{4} \times \frac{9}{2} = \frac{27}{8}$$

Check Your Skills

Evaluate the following expressions. Simplify all fractions.

11. $\dfrac{1}{6} \div \dfrac{1}{11} =$

12. $\dfrac{8}{5} \div \dfrac{4}{15} =$

Answers can be found on page 42.

Fractions in Equations

When an x appears in a fraction multiplication or division problem, we'll use essentially the same concepts and techniques to solve.

$$\frac{4}{3}x = \frac{15}{8}$$

Divide both sides by $\dfrac{4}{3}$:

$$x = \frac{15}{8} \div \frac{4}{3}$$

$$x = \frac{15}{8} \times \frac{3}{4} = \frac{45}{32}$$

An important tool to add to our arsenal at this point is *cross-multiplication*. This tool comes from the principle of making common denominators.

$$\frac{x}{7} = \frac{5}{8}$$

The common denominator of 7 and 8 is $7 \times 8 = 56$. So we have to multiply the left fraction by 8/8 and the right fraction by 7/7:

$$\frac{8 \times x}{8 \times 7} = \frac{5 \times 7}{8 \times 7}$$

Now we can set the numerators equal: $8x = 5 \times 7 = 35$
$$x = 35/8$$

However, in this situation we can avoid having to determine the common denominator by cross–multiplying each numerator times the other denominator and setting the products equal to each other.

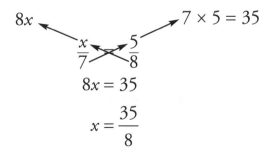

$$8x = 35$$

$$x = \frac{35}{8}$$

Check Your Skills

Solve for x in the following equations.

13. $\dfrac{3}{4}x = \dfrac{3}{2}$

14. $\dfrac{x}{6} = \dfrac{5}{3}$

Answers can be found on page 42.

Switching Between Improper Fractions and Mixed Numbers

Let's return to our discussion of why 5/4 equals $1^1/4$ and how to switch between improper fractions and mixed numbers.

To do this we need to talk about the numerator in more detail. The numerator is a description of how many parts you have. The fraction 5/4 tells us that we have 5 parts. But we have some flexibility in how we arrange those 5 parts. For instance, we already expressed it above as 4/4 + 1/4, or 1 + 1/4. Essentially what we did was we split the numerator into two pieces: 4 and 1. If we wanted to express this as a fraction, we could say that 5/4 becomes $\dfrac{4+1}{4}$. This hasn't changed anything, because 4 + 1 equals 5, so we still have the same number of parts.

Then, as we saw above, we can split our fraction into two separate fractions. For instance $\dfrac{4+1}{4}$ becomes $\dfrac{4}{4} + \dfrac{1}{4}$. This is the same as saying that 5 fourths equals 4 fourths plus 1 fourth. So we have several different ways of representing the same fraction. $\dfrac{5}{4} = \dfrac{4+1}{4} = \dfrac{4}{4} + \dfrac{1}{4}$. Here is a visual representation:

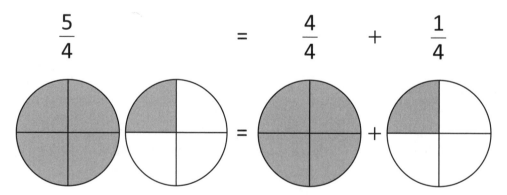

As a general rule, we can always split the numerator into different parts and split a fraction into multiple fractions. This is just reversing the process of adding fractions. When we add fractions, we take two fractions with the same denominator and combine them into one fraction. Here we are doing the exact opposite—turning one fraction into two separate fractions, each with the same denominator. And now that our fraction 5/4 is split into two fractions, we can take advantage of the fact that fractions, at their essence, represent division. As we discussed earlier, 4/4 = 1. Our original explanation didn't mention division, but as we mentioned above, another way to think of 4/4 is 4 ÷ 4, which equals 1.

To switch from an improper fraction to a mixed number, we want to figure out how many complete units we have. To do that, we need to figure out the largest multiple of the denominator that is less than or equal to the numerator. For the fraction 5/4, 4 is the largest multiple of 4 that is less than 5. So we split our fraction into 4/4 and 1/4. We then note that 4/4 equals 1, so our mixed number is $1^{1}/_{4}$.

Let's try it again with the fraction 15/4. This time, the largest multiple of 4 that is less than 15 is 12. So we can split our fraction 15/4 into 12/4 + 3/4. In other words, $\frac{15}{4} = \frac{12+3}{4} = \frac{12}{4} + \frac{3}{4}$. And 12/4 = 3, so the fraction 15/4 becomes the mixed number $3^{3}/_{4}$.

Let's try one with a different denominator. How do we turn the fraction 16/7 into a mixed number? This time we need the largest multiple of 7 that is less than or equal to 16. 14 is the largest multiple of 7 less than 16, so we once again split our fraction 16/7 into 14/7 and 2/7.

$\frac{16}{7} = \frac{14+2}{7} = \frac{14}{7} + \frac{2}{7}$. 14 divided by 7 equals 2, so our mixed number is $2^{2}/_{7}$.

Check Your Skills

Change the following improper fractions to mixed numbers.

15. $\dfrac{11}{6}$

16. $\dfrac{100}{11}$

Answers can be found on page 42.

Changing Mixed Numbers to Improper Fractions

Now that we know how to change a number from an improper fraction to a mixed number, we also need to be able to do the reverse. Suppose we have the mixed number $5^{2}/_{3}$. How do we turn this number into a fraction?

To do so, we need to remember that we can think of any number (even an integer) as a fraction. The number 1, for instance, can be thought of any number of different ways. It can be thought of as 1/1. It can also be thought of as 2/2. In other words, a unit circle has been split into 2 equal pieces, and we have 2 of those pieces (forming a single whole again). 1 can also be written as 3/3, 4/4, 5/5, etc.

In fact, we can think of the process of turning mixed numbers into improper fractions as simple fraction addition. $5^{2}/_{3}$ is the same thing as 5 + 2/3, so we can think of it as $\frac{5}{1} + \frac{2}{3}$. Now we know what to do—we need to change $\frac{5}{1}$ so that it has a denominator of 3. The way to do that is to multiply $\frac{5}{1}$ by $\frac{3}{3}$.

$5 = \frac{5}{1} = \frac{5}{1} \times \frac{3}{3} = \frac{5 \times 3}{1 \times 3} = \frac{15}{3}$. So our mixed number is really $\frac{15}{3} + \frac{2}{3} = \frac{15+2}{3} = \frac{17}{3}$.

Check Your Skills

Change the following mixed numbers to improper fractions.

17. $3\frac{3}{4}$

18. $5\frac{2}{3}$

Answers can be found on page 42.

Division in Disguise

Sometimes, dividing fractions can be written in a confusing way. Consider one of the previous examples:

$\frac{1}{2} \div \frac{3}{4}$ can also be written as a "double–decker" fraction this way: $\dfrac{\dfrac{1}{2}}{\dfrac{3}{4}}$

Do not be confused. You can rewrite this as the top fraction divided by the bottom fraction, and solve it normally (by using the reciprocal of the bottom fraction and then multiplying).

$$\frac{\dfrac{1}{2}}{\dfrac{3}{4}} = \frac{1}{2} \div \frac{3}{4} = \frac{1}{2} \times \frac{4}{3} = \frac{4}{6} = \frac{2}{3}$$

Also notice that you can often simplify quickly by multiplying both top and bottom by a common denominator:

$$\frac{\dfrac{1}{2}}{\dfrac{3}{4}} = \frac{\dfrac{1}{2} \times 4}{\dfrac{3}{4} \times 4} = \frac{2}{3}$$

Check Your Skills

19. $\dfrac{\dfrac{3}{5}}{\dfrac{2}{3}} = ?$

20. $\dfrac{\dfrac{5}{7}}{\dfrac{1}{4}} = ?$

Answers can be found on page 42.

Fraction Operations: Funky Results

Adding and subtracting fractions leads to expected results. When you add two positive fractions, you get a larger number. When you subtract a positive fraction from something else, you get a smaller number.

However, multiplying by proper fractions (fractions between 0 and 1) yields UNEXPECTED results.

$$9 \times \frac{1}{3} = 3 \qquad\qquad\qquad 3 < 9$$

Multiplying a number by a proper fraction creates a product SMALLER than the original number. (We're talking about positive fractions here.) Note that this is also true when the original number is a fraction.

$$\frac{1}{2} \times \frac{1}{4} = \frac{1}{8} \qquad\qquad\qquad \frac{1}{8} < \frac{1}{2}$$

Similarly, dividing by a proper fraction yields a quotient that is LARGER than the original number.

$$\frac{6}{\frac{3}{4}} = 6 \div \frac{3}{4} = 6 \times \frac{4}{3} = \frac{24}{3} = 8 \qquad\qquad 8 > 6$$

This is also true when the original number is a fraction.

$$\frac{\frac{1}{4}}{\frac{5}{6}} = \frac{1}{4} \div \frac{5}{6} = \frac{1}{4} \times \frac{6}{5} = \frac{6}{20} = \frac{3}{10} \qquad\qquad \frac{3}{10} > \frac{1}{4}$$

Check Your Skills

21. $\dfrac{1}{2} \times \dfrac{1}{4} = ?$

22. $\dfrac{1}{2} \div \dfrac{1}{4} = ?$

Answers can be found on page 42.

Comparing Fractions: Cross-Multiply

Which fraction is greater, $\dfrac{7}{9}$ or $\dfrac{4}{5}$?

The traditional method of comparing fractions involves finding a common denominator and comparing the two fractions. The common denominator of 9 and 5 is 45.

Thus, $\dfrac{7}{9} = \dfrac{35}{45}$ and $\dfrac{4}{5} = \dfrac{36}{45}$. We can see that $\dfrac{4}{5}$ is slightly bigger than $\dfrac{7}{9}$.

However, there is a shortcut to comparing fractions called cross–multiplication. This is a process that involves multiplying the numerator of one fraction with the denominator of the other fraction, and vice versa:

$$\dfrac{7}{9} \qquad\qquad \dfrac{4}{5}$$ Set up the fractions next to each other.

$$\begin{array}{cc} (7 \times 5) & (4 \times 9) \\ 35 & 36 \end{array}$$ Cross–multiply the fractions and put each answer by the corresponding <u>numerator</u> (NOT the denominator!)

$$\dfrac{7}{9} \quad < \quad \dfrac{4}{5}$$ Since 35 is less than 36, the first fraction must be less than the second one.

Check Your Skills

23. Which fraction is greater? $\dfrac{4}{13}$ or $\dfrac{1}{3}$?

24. Which fraction is smaller? $\dfrac{5}{9}$ or $\dfrac{8}{13}$?

Answers can be found on page 42–43.

Never Split the Denominator

One final rule, perhaps the most important one, is one that you must always remember when working with complex fractions. A complex fraction is a fraction in which there is a sum or a difference in the numerator or the denominator. Three examples of complex fractions are:

(a) $\dfrac{15+10}{5}$ (b) $\dfrac{5}{15+10}$ (c) $\dfrac{15+10}{5+2}$

In example (a), the numerator is expressed as a sum.
In example (b), the denominator is expressed as a sum.
In example (c), both the numerator and the denominator are expressed as sums.

When simplifying fractions that incorporate sums or differences, remember this rule: You may split up the terms of the numerator, but you may NEVER split the terms of the DENOMINATOR.

Thus, the terms in example (a) may be split:

$$\dfrac{15+10}{5} = \dfrac{15}{5} + \dfrac{10}{5} = 3 + 2 = 5$$

But the terms in example (b) may not be split:

$$\dfrac{5}{15+10} \neq \dfrac{5}{15} + \dfrac{5}{10} \quad \textbf{NO!}$$

Instead, simplify the denominator first:

$$\frac{5}{15+10} = \frac{5}{25} = \frac{1}{5}$$

The terms in example (c) may not be split either:

$$\frac{15+10}{5+2} \neq \frac{15}{5} + \frac{10}{2} \quad \textbf{NO!}$$

Instead, simplify both parts of the fraction:

$$\frac{15+10}{5} = \frac{25}{7} = 3\frac{4}{7}$$

Often, GRE problems will involve complex fractions with variables. On these problems, it is tempting to split the denominator. Do not fall for it!

It is tempting to perform the following simplification:

$$\frac{\mathbf{5x-2y}}{\mathbf{x-y}} = \frac{5x}{x} - \frac{2y}{y} = 5 - 2 = 3$$

But this is **WRONG** because you cannot split terms in the denominator.

The reality is that $\dfrac{5x-2y}{x-y}$ cannot be simplified further.

On the other hand, the expression $\dfrac{\mathbf{6x-15y}}{\mathbf{10}}$ can be simplified by splitting the difference, because this difference appears in the numerator.

$$\text{Thus:} \quad \frac{6x-15y}{10} = \frac{6x}{10} - \frac{15y}{10} = \frac{3x}{5} - \frac{3y}{2}$$

Check Your Skills

25. $\dfrac{13+7}{5}$

26. $\dfrac{21+6}{7+6}$

27. $\dfrac{48a-12b}{a-b}$

Answers can be found on page 43.

Benchmark Values

You will use a variety of estimating strategies on the GRE. One important strategy for estimating with fractions is to use Benchmark Values. These are simple fractions with which you are already familiar:

$$\frac{1}{10}, \frac{1}{5}, \frac{1}{4}, \frac{1}{3}, \frac{1}{2}, \frac{2}{3}, \text{ and } \frac{3}{4}$$

You can use Benchmark Values to compare fractions:

Which is greater: $\dfrac{127}{255}$ or $\dfrac{162}{320}$?

If you recognize that 127 is less than half of 255, and 162 is more than half of 320, you will save yourself a lot of cumbersome computation.

You can also use Benchmark Values to estimate computations involving fractions:

What is $\dfrac{10}{22}$ of $\dfrac{5}{18}$ of 2,000, approximately?

If you recognize that these fractions are very close to the Benchmark Values $\dfrac{1}{2}$ and $\dfrac{1}{4}$, you can estimate:

$\dfrac{1}{2}$ of $\dfrac{1}{4}$ of 2,000 = 250. Therefore, $\dfrac{10}{22}$ of $\dfrac{5}{18}$ of 2,000 ≈ 250.

Notice that the rounding errors compensated for each other.

$\dfrac{10}{22} \approx \dfrac{10}{20} = \dfrac{1}{2}$ You decreased the denominator, so you rounded up: $\dfrac{10}{22} < \dfrac{1}{2}$

$\dfrac{5}{18} \approx \dfrac{5}{20} = \dfrac{1}{4}$ You increased the denominator, so you rounded down: $\dfrac{5}{18} > \dfrac{1}{4}$

If you had rounded $\dfrac{5}{18}$ to $\dfrac{6}{18} = \dfrac{1}{3}$ instead, then you would have rounded **both** fractions up. This would lead to a slight but systematic overestimation.

$$\frac{1}{2} \times \frac{1}{3} \times 2000 \approx 333$$

Try to make your rounding errors cancel by rounding some numbers up and others down.

Check Your Skills

28. Which is greater: $\dfrac{123}{250}$ or $\dfrac{171}{340}$?

29. Approximate $\left(\dfrac{15}{58}\right)\left(\dfrac{9}{19}\right)403$

Answers can be found on page 43.

Smart Numbers: Multiples of the Denominators

Sometimes, fraction problems on the GRE include unspecified numerical amounts; often these unspecified amounts are described by variables. In these cases, pick real numbers to stand in for the variables. To make the computation easier, choose **Smart Numbers** equal to common multiples of the denominators of the fractions in the problem.

For example, consider this problem:

> The Crandalls' hot tub is half-filled. Their swimming pool, which has a capacity four times that of the tub, is filled to four-fifths of its capacity. If the hot tub is drained into the swimming pool, to what fraction of its capacity will the pool be filled?

The denominators in this problem are 2 (from 1/2 for the hot tub) and 5 (from 4/5 for the pool). The Smart Number in this case is the least common denominator, which is 10. Therefore, assign the hot tub a capacity of 10 units. Since the swimming pool has a capacity 4 times that of the pool, the swimming pool has a capacity of 40 units. We know that the hot tub is only half-filled; therefore, it has 5 units of water in it. The swimming pool is four-fifths of the way filled, so it has 32 units of water in it.

Let us add the 5 units of water from the hot tub to the 32 units of water that are already in the swimming pool: $32 + 5 = 37$.

With 37 units of water and a total capacity of 40, the pool will be filled to $\dfrac{37}{40}$ of its total capacity.

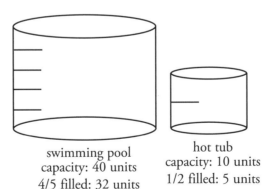

swimming pool
capacity: 40 units
4/5 filled: 32 units

hot tub
capacity: 10 units
1/2 filled: 5 units

Check Your Skills

30. Mili's first generation uHear is filled to 1/2 capacity with songs. Her second generation uHear, which has 3 times the capacity of her first generation uHear, is at 4/5 capacity. Will Mili be able to transfer all of her music from her first generation uHear to her second generation uHear?

Answers can be found on page 43.

When Not to Use Smart Numbers

In some problems, even though an amount might be unknown to you, it is actually specified in the problem in another way. In these cases, you cannot use Smart Numbers to assign real numbers to the variables. For example, consider this problem:

Mark's comic book collection contains 1/3 Killer Fish comics and 3/8 Shazaam Woman comics. The remainder of his collection consists of Boom! comics. If Mark has 70 Boom! comics, how many comics does he have in his entire collection?

Even though you do not know the number of comics in Mark's collection, you can see that the total is not completely unspecified. You know a piece of the total: 70 Boom! comics. You can use this information to find the total. Do not use Smart Numbers here. Instead, solve similar problems by figuring out how big the known piece is; then, use that knowledge to find the size of the whole. You will need to set up an equation and solve:

$$\frac{1}{3} \text{ Killer Fish } + \frac{3}{8} \text{ Shazaam Woman } = \frac{17}{24} \text{ comics that are not Boom!}$$

Therefore, $\dfrac{24}{24} - \dfrac{17}{24} = \dfrac{7}{24}$ of the comics are in fact Boom! comics.

$$\frac{7}{24}x = 70$$

$$x = 70 \times \frac{24}{7}$$

$$x = 240$$

Mark has 240 comics.

In summary, **do** pick smart numbers when no amounts are given in the problem, but **do not** pick smart numbers when *any* amount or total is given!

Check Your Skills

31. If John spends 1/3 of his waking hours working, 1/5 eating meals, 3/10 at the gym, and 2 hours going to and from work, how many hours is John awake?

Answers can be found on page 43–44.

Check Your Skills Answers

1. $\dfrac{5}{7}, \dfrac{3}{7}$: The denominators of the two fractions are the same, but the numerator of $\dfrac{5}{7}$ is bigger, so $\dfrac{5}{7} > \dfrac{3}{7}$.

2. $\dfrac{3}{10}, \dfrac{3}{13}$: The numerators of the two fractions are the same, but the denominator of $\dfrac{3}{10}$ is smaller, so

$$\dfrac{3}{10} > \dfrac{3}{13}.$$

3. $\dfrac{5}{4}$: $\dfrac{1}{2} + \dfrac{3}{4} = \dfrac{1}{2} \times \dfrac{2}{2} + \dfrac{3}{4} = \dfrac{2}{4} + \dfrac{3}{4} = \dfrac{2+3}{4} = \dfrac{5}{4}$ (you have five quarters of a pie)

4. $\dfrac{7}{24}$: $\dfrac{2}{3} - \dfrac{3}{8} = \dfrac{2}{3} \times \dfrac{8}{8} - \dfrac{3}{8} \times \dfrac{3}{3} = \dfrac{16}{24} - \dfrac{9}{24} = \dfrac{16-9}{24} = \dfrac{7}{24}$

5. **11** : $\dfrac{x}{5} + \dfrac{2}{5} = \dfrac{13}{5}$

$$\dfrac{x}{5} = \dfrac{13}{5} - \dfrac{2}{5}$$

$$\dfrac{x}{5} = \dfrac{11}{5}$$

$$x = 11$$

6. **4** : $\dfrac{x}{3} - \dfrac{4}{9} = \dfrac{8}{9}$

$$\dfrac{x}{3} = \dfrac{8}{9} + \dfrac{4}{9}$$

$$\dfrac{x}{3} = \dfrac{12}{9}$$

$$\dfrac{x}{3} \times \dfrac{3}{3} = \dfrac{12}{9}$$

$$\dfrac{3x}{9} = \dfrac{12}{9}$$

$$3x = 12$$

$$x = 4$$

7. $\dfrac{5}{8}$: $\dfrac{25}{40} = \dfrac{5 \times 5}{8 \times 5} = \dfrac{5 \times \cancel{5}}{8 \times \cancel{5}} = \dfrac{5}{8}$

8. $\dfrac{2}{3}$: $\dfrac{16}{24} = \dfrac{2 \times 8}{3 \times 8} = \dfrac{2 \times \cancel{8}}{3 \times \cancel{8}} = \dfrac{2}{3}$

9. $\dfrac{9}{35}$: $\dfrac{3}{7} \times \dfrac{6}{10} = \dfrac{3}{7} \times \dfrac{3}{5} = \dfrac{9}{35}$

10. $\dfrac{1}{8}$: $\dfrac{5}{14} \times \dfrac{7}{20} = \dfrac{5}{2 \times 7} \times \dfrac{7}{4 \times 5} = \dfrac{\cancel{5}}{2 \times \cancel{7}} \times \dfrac{\cancel{7}}{4 \times \cancel{5}} = \dfrac{1}{8}$

11. $\dfrac{\mathbf{11}}{\mathbf{6}}$: $\dfrac{1}{6} \div \dfrac{1}{11} = \dfrac{1}{6} \times \dfrac{11}{1} = \dfrac{11}{6}$

12. **6** : $\dfrac{8}{5} \div \dfrac{4}{15} = \dfrac{8}{5} \times \dfrac{15}{4} = \dfrac{2 \times 4}{5} \times \dfrac{3 \times 5}{4} = \dfrac{2 \times \cancel{4}}{\cancel{5}} \times \dfrac{3 \times \cancel{5}}{\cancel{4}} = \dfrac{6}{1} = 6$

13. **2** : $\dfrac{3}{4}x = \dfrac{3}{2}$

     $x = \dfrac{3}{2} \div \dfrac{3}{4} = \dfrac{3}{2} \times \dfrac{4}{3}$

     $x = \dfrac{3 \times 2 \times 2}{2 \times 3} = \dfrac{\cancel{3} \times \cancel{2} \times 2}{\cancel{2} \times \cancel{3}} = \dfrac{2}{1}$

     $x = 2$

14. **10** : $\dfrac{x}{6} = \dfrac{5}{3}$

     $3 \times x = 5 \times 6$

     $3x = 30$

     $x = 10$

15. $\mathbf{1\tfrac{5}{6}}$: $\dfrac{11}{6} = \dfrac{6+5}{6} = \dfrac{6}{6} + \dfrac{5}{6} = 1 + \dfrac{5}{6} = 1\tfrac{5}{6}$

16. $\mathbf{9\tfrac{1}{11}}$: $\dfrac{100}{11} = \dfrac{99+1}{11} = \dfrac{99}{11} + \dfrac{1}{11} = 9 + \dfrac{1}{11} = 9\tfrac{1}{11}$

17. $\dfrac{\mathbf{15}}{\mathbf{4}}$: $3\tfrac{3}{4} = 3 + \dfrac{3}{4} = \dfrac{3}{1} \times \dfrac{4}{4} + \dfrac{3}{4} = \dfrac{12}{4} + \dfrac{3}{4} = \dfrac{15}{4}$

18. $\dfrac{\mathbf{17}}{\mathbf{3}}$: $5\tfrac{2}{3} = 5 + \dfrac{2}{3} = \dfrac{5}{1} \times \dfrac{3}{3} + \dfrac{2}{3} = \dfrac{15}{3} + \dfrac{2}{3} = \dfrac{17}{3}$

19. $\dfrac{\mathbf{9}}{\mathbf{10}}$: $\dfrac{\tfrac{3}{5}}{\tfrac{2}{3}} = \dfrac{3}{5} \times \dfrac{3}{2} = \dfrac{9}{10}$

20. $\dfrac{\mathbf{20}}{\mathbf{7}}$: $\dfrac{\tfrac{5}{7}}{\tfrac{1}{4}} = \dfrac{5}{7} \times \dfrac{4}{1} = \dfrac{20}{7}$

21. $\dfrac{\mathbf{1}}{\mathbf{8}}$: $\dfrac{1}{2} \times \dfrac{1}{4} = \dfrac{1}{8}$

22. **2** : $\dfrac{1}{2} \div \dfrac{1}{4} = \dfrac{1}{2} \times \dfrac{4}{1} = \dfrac{4}{2} = 2$

       $3 \times 4 = 12$ $13 \times 1 = 13$

23. $\dfrac{\mathbf{1}}{\mathbf{13}}$: $\dfrac{4}{13} \bowtie \dfrac{1}{3}$ $\dfrac{1}{3}$ is greater than $\dfrac{4}{13}$.

$$5 \times 13 = 65 \qquad 8 \times 9 = 72$$

24. $\dfrac{5}{9}$: $\qquad \dfrac{5}{9} \diagdown \dfrac{8}{13} \qquad \dfrac{5}{9}$ is smaller than $\dfrac{8}{13}$.

25. **4:** Add the numerator and simplify. $\dfrac{13 + 7}{5} = \dfrac{20}{5} = 4$.

26. $2\dfrac{1}{13}$: Add the numerator and the denominator. $\dfrac{21 + 6}{7 + 6} = \dfrac{27}{13} = 2\dfrac{1}{13}$.

27. $\dfrac{12(4a - b)}{a - b}$: The only thing you can do is factor 12 out of the numerator. $\dfrac{48a - 12b}{a - b} = \dfrac{12(4a - b)}{a - b}$.

No further simplification is possible.

28. $\dfrac{171}{340}$: $\dfrac{123}{250}$ is a little less than $\dfrac{125}{250}$, and so is less than $\dfrac{1}{2}$.

$\dfrac{171}{340}$ is a little more than $\dfrac{170}{340}$, and so is less than $\dfrac{1}{2}$.

$\dfrac{171}{340}$ is greater than $\dfrac{123}{250}$.

29. **50:** Approximate each term. $\dfrac{15}{58} \approx \dfrac{15}{60} \approx \dfrac{1}{4}$, $\dfrac{9}{19} \approx \dfrac{9}{18} \approx \dfrac{1}{2}$, and 403 is close to 400.

$\left(\dfrac{15}{58}\right)\left(\dfrac{9}{19}\right)403 \approx \left(\dfrac{1}{4}\right)\left(\dfrac{1}{2}\right)400 \approx 50$.

30. **Yes:** Since we are only given fractions, pick numbers. 10 is a good number because it is the common denominator of the fractions 1/2 and 4/5. Her 1st generation uHear has a capacity of 10 gigabytes. Her 2nd generation uHear, then, has a capacity of 30 gigabytes.

Her 1st generation uHear then has 5 gigabytes (1/2 × 10) and her 2nd generation uHear has 24 gigabytes (4/5 × 30). If she transferred the songs on the 1st uHear to the 2nd, she would be at 29/30 capacity. There is still room.

30. **12 hours:** Because we are given an actual number in the problem, we are not allowed to pick numbers. We should assign a variable for what we are looking for: the number of hours John is awake. Let's call that total x.

Therefore, our equation will be $\dfrac{1}{3}x + \dfrac{1}{5}x + \dfrac{3}{10}x + 2 = x$

The common denominator of all the fractions is 30. Multiply the equation by 30 to eliminate all the fractions.

$$30\left(\frac{1}{3}x + \frac{1}{5}x + \frac{3}{10}x + 2\right) = (x)30$$

$$10x + 6x + 9x + 60 = 30x$$

$$25x + 60 = 30x$$

$$60 = 5x$$

$$12 = x$$

John is awake for 12 hours.

Problem Set

For problems #1–5, decide whether the given operation will yield an INCREASE, a DECREASE, or a result that will STAY THE SAME.

1.   Multiply the numerator of a positive, proper fraction by $\dfrac{3}{2}$.

2.   Add 1 to the numerator of a positive, proper fraction and subtract 1 from its denominator.

3.   Multiply both the numerator and denominator of a positive, proper fraction by $3\dfrac{1}{2}$.

4.   Multiply a positive, proper fraction by $\dfrac{3}{8}$.

5.   Divide a positive, proper fraction by $\dfrac{3}{13}$.

Solve problems #6–15.

6.   Simplify: $\dfrac{10x}{5+x}$

7.   Simplify: $\dfrac{8(3)(x)^2(3)}{6x}$

8.   Simplify: $\dfrac{\dfrac{3}{5}+\dfrac{1}{3}}{\dfrac{2}{3}+\dfrac{2}{5}}$

9.   Simplify: $\dfrac{12ab^3-6a^2b}{3ab}$ (given that $ab \neq 0$)

10.   Put these fractions in order from least to greatest: $\dfrac{9}{17}, \dfrac{3}{16}, \dfrac{19}{20}, \dfrac{7}{15}$

11.   Put these fractions in order from least to greatest: $\dfrac{2}{3}, \dfrac{3}{13}, \dfrac{5}{7}, \dfrac{2}{9}$

12. Lisa spends $\frac{3}{8}$ of her monthly paycheck on rent and $\frac{5}{12}$ on food. Her roommate, Carrie, who earns twice as much as Lisa, spends $\frac{1}{4}$ of her monthly paycheck on rent and $\frac{1}{2}$ on food. If the two women decide to donate the remainder of their money to charity each month, what fraction of their combined monthly income will they donate?

13. Rob spends $\frac{1}{2}$ of his monthly paycheck, after taxes, on rent. He spends $\frac{1}{3}$ on food and $\frac{1}{8}$ on entertainment. If he donates the entire remainder, $500, to charity, what is Rob's monthly income, after taxes?

14. Are $\frac{\sqrt{3}}{2}$ and $\frac{2\sqrt{3}}{3}$ reciprocals?

15. Estimate to the closest integer: What is $\frac{11}{30}$ of $\frac{6}{20}$ of 120?

16.

Column A	**Column B**
$\frac{2}{3} \times \frac{3}{3}$	$\frac{2}{3} \times \frac{4}{4}$

17.

Column A	**Column B**
$\dfrac{6x+6y}{3x+y}$	8

18.

An 18 oz glass is filled with 8 oz of orange juice. More orange juice is added so the glass is 5/6 full

Column A	**Column B**
Amount of orange juice added	6 oz.

1. **INCREASE:** Multiplying the numerator of a positive fraction increases the numerator. As the numerator of a positive, proper fraction increases, its value increases.

2. **INCREASE:** As the numerator of a positive, proper fraction increases, the value of the fraction increases. As the denominator of a positive, proper fraction decreases, the value of the fraction also increases. Both actions will work to increase the value of the fraction.

3. **STAY THE SAME:** Multiplying or dividing the numerator and denominator of a fraction by the same number will not change the value of the fraction.

4. **DECREASE:** Multiplying a positive number by a proper fraction decreases the number.

5. **INCREASE:** Dividing a positive number by a positive, proper fraction increases the number.

6. **CANNOT SIMPLIFY:** There is no way to simplify this fraction; it is already in simplest form. Remember, you cannot split the denominator!

7. **12x:** First, cancel terms in both the numerator and the denominator. Then combine terms.

$$\frac{8(3)(x)^2(3)}{6x} = \frac{8(\cancel{3})(x)^2(3)}{\cancel{6}2x} = \frac{\cancel{8}4(x)^2(3)}{\cancel{2}x} = \frac{4(x)^{\cancel{2}}(3)}{\cancel{x}} = 4(x)(3) = 12x$$

8. **$\dfrac{7}{8}$:** First, add the fractions in the numerator and denominator. This results in $\dfrac{14}{15}$ and $\dfrac{16}{15}$, respectively.

To save time, multiply each of the small fractions by 15, which is the common denominator of all the fractions in the problem. Because we are multiplying the numerator *and* the denominator of the whole complex fraction by 15, we are not changing its value.

$$\frac{9+5}{10+6} = \frac{14}{16} = \frac{7}{8}$$

9. **$2(2b^2 - a)$ or $4b^2 - 2a$:** First, factor out common terms in the numerator. Then, cancel terms in both the numerator and denominator.

$$\frac{6ab(2b^2 - a)}{3ab} = 2(2b^2 - a) \text{ or } 4b^2 - 2a$$

10. $\dfrac{3}{16} < \dfrac{7}{15} < \dfrac{9}{17} < \dfrac{19}{20}$ **:** Use Benchmark Values to compare these fractions.

$\dfrac{9}{17}$ is slightly more than $\dfrac{1}{2}$. $\dfrac{3}{16}$ is slightly less than $\dfrac{1}{4}$.

$\dfrac{19}{20}$ is slightly less than 1. $\dfrac{7}{15}$ is slightly less than $\dfrac{1}{2}$.

This makes it easy to order the fractions: $\dfrac{3}{16} < \dfrac{7}{15} < \dfrac{9}{17} < \dfrac{19}{20}$.

11. $\dfrac{2}{9} < \dfrac{3}{13} < \dfrac{2}{3} < \dfrac{5}{7}$: Using Benchmark Values, you should notice that $\dfrac{3}{13}$ and $\dfrac{2}{9}$ are both less than $\dfrac{1}{2}$.

$\dfrac{2}{3}$ and $\dfrac{5}{7}$ are both more than $\dfrac{1}{2}$. Use cross–multiplication to compare each pair of fractions:

$$3 \times 9 = 27 \qquad \dfrac{3}{13} \diagdown\!\!\!\!\diagup \dfrac{2}{9} \qquad 2 \times 13 = 26 \qquad\qquad \dfrac{3}{13} > \dfrac{2}{9}$$

$$2 \times 7 = 14 \qquad \dfrac{2}{3} \diagdown\!\!\!\!\diagup \dfrac{5}{7} \qquad 5 \times 3 = 15 \qquad\qquad \dfrac{2}{3} > \dfrac{5}{7}$$

This makes it easy to order the fractions: $\dfrac{2}{9} < \dfrac{3}{13} < \dfrac{2}{3} < \dfrac{5}{7}$.

12. $\dfrac{17}{72}$: Use Smart Numbers to solve this problem. Since the denominators in the problem are 8, 12, 4,

and 2, assign Lisa a monthly paycheck of $24. Assign her roommate, who earns twice as much, a monthly paycheck of $48. The two women's monthly expenses break down as follows:

	Rent	Food	Leftover
Lisa	$\dfrac{3}{8}$ of 24 = 9	$\dfrac{5}{12}$ of 24 = 10	24 − (9 + 10) = 5
Carrie	$\dfrac{1}{4}$ of 48 = 12	$\dfrac{1}{2}$ of 48 = 24	48 − (12 + 24) = 12

The women will donate a total of $17, out of their combined monthly income of $72.

13. **$12,000:** You cannot use Smart Numbers in this problem, because the total amount is specified. Even though the exact figure is not given in the problem, a portion of the total is specified. This means that the total is a certain number, although you do not know what it is. In fact, the total is exactly what you are being asked to find. Clearly, if you assign a number to represent the total, you will not be able to accurately find the total.

First, use addition to find the fraction of Rob's money that he spends on rent, food, and entertainment:

$\dfrac{1}{2} + \dfrac{1}{3} + \dfrac{1}{8} = \dfrac{12}{24} + \dfrac{8}{24} + \dfrac{3}{24} = \dfrac{23}{24}$. Therefore, the $500 that he donates to charity represents $\dfrac{1}{24}$ of his total

monthly paycheck. We can set up a proportion: $\dfrac{500}{x} = \dfrac{1}{24}$. Thus, Rob's monthly income is $500 × 24, or

$12,000.

14. **YES:** The product of a number and its reciprocal must equal 1. To test whether or not two numbers are reciprocals, multiply them. If the product is 1, they are reciprocals; if it is not, they are not:

$$\frac{\sqrt{3}}{2} \times \frac{2\sqrt{3}}{3} = \frac{2\left(\sqrt{3}\right)^2}{2(3)} = \frac{6}{6} = 1$$

The numbers are indeed reciprocals.

15. **Approximately 13:** Use Benchmark Values to estimate: $\frac{11}{30}$ is slightly more than $\frac{1}{3}$. $\frac{6}{20}$ is slightly less than $\frac{1}{3}$. Therefore, $\frac{11}{30}$ of $\frac{6}{20}$ of 120 should be approximately $\frac{1}{3}$ of $\frac{1}{3}$ of 120, or $\frac{120}{9}$, which is slightly more than 13. (A third of 120 is 40; a third of 40 is a little over 13.)

Another technique to solve this problem would be to write the product and cancel common factors:

$$\frac{11}{30} \times \frac{6}{20} \times 120 = \frac{(11)(6)(120)}{(30)(20)} = \frac{(11)(\cancel{6})(120)}{(\cancel{30}5)(20)} = \frac{(11)(\cancel{120}6)}{(5)(\cancel{20})} = \frac{66}{5} = 13.2$$

Note that for estimation problems, there is no "correct" answer. The key is to arrive at an estimate that is close to the exact answer—and to do so quickly!

16. **C:** 3/3 and 4/4 are both equal to 1. Each column can be rewritten as 2/3 × 1, which leaves you with 2/3.

Column A	**Column B**
$\frac{2}{3} \cdot \frac{3}{3} =$	$\frac{2}{3} \cdot \frac{4}{4} =$
$\frac{2}{3} \cdot 1 =$	$\frac{2}{3} \cdot 1 =$
$\frac{2}{3}$	$\frac{2}{3}$

17. **D:** When you are adding you cannot split the denominator. Therefore the most that you can simplify Column A is $\frac{6(x+y)}{3x+y}$. But that isn't enough to tell you whether the value of this expression is more or less than 8.

18. **A:** The easiest way to solve this problem is to find out how much liquid is in the glass after the orange juice is added. The glass is 5/6 full, and 5/6 × 18 = 15. There are 15 ounces of orange juice. There were 8 ounces of OJ, so 7 ounces were added.

An 18 oz glass is filled with 8 oz of orange juice. More orange juice is added so the glass is 5/6 full

Column A

Amount of orange juice added

= 7 oz.

Column B

6 oz.

Chapter 2
of
FRACTIONS, DECIMALS, & PERCENTS

DIGITS &
DECIMALS

In This Chapter . . .

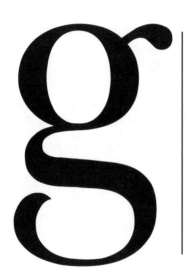

- Place Value
- Adding Zeroes to Decimals
- Powers of 10: Shifting the Decimal
- The Heavy Division Shortcut
- Decimal Operations

DECIMALS

GRE math goes beyond an understanding of the properties of integers (which include the counting numbers, such as 1, 2, 3, their negative counterparts, such as −1, −2, −3, and 0). The GRE also tests your ability to understand the numbers that fall in between the integers. Such numbers can be expressed as decimals. For example, the decimal 6.3 falls between the integers 6 and 7.

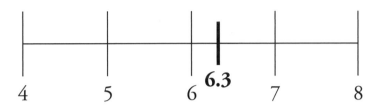

Some other examples of decimals include:

Decimals less than −1:   −3.65, −12.01, −145.9
Decimals between −1 and 0:   −0.65, −0.8912, −0.076
Decimals between 0 and 1:   0.65, 0.8912, 0.076
Decimals greater than 1:   3.65, 12.01, 145.9

Note that an integer can be expressed as a decimal by adding the decimal point and the digit 0. For example:

$$8 = 8.0 \qquad -123 = -123.0 \qquad 400 = 400.0$$

DIGITS

Every number is composed of digits. There are only ten digits in our number system: 0, 1, 2, 3, 4, 5, 6, 7, 8, 9. The term digit refers to one building block of a number; it does not refer to a number itself. For example: 356 is a number composed of three digits: 3, 5, and 6.

Integers can be classified by the number of digits they contain. For example:

2, 7, and −8 are each single-digit numbers (they are each composed of one digit).
43, 63, and −14 are each double-digit numbers (composed of two digits).
500,000 and −468,024 are each six-digit numbers (composed of six digits).
789,526,622 is a nine-digit number (composed of nine digits).

Non-integers are not generally classified by the number of digits they contain, since you can always add any number of zeroes at the end, on the right side of the decimal point:

$$9.1 = 9.10 = 9.100$$

Place Value

Every digit in a number has a particular place value depending on its location within the number. For example, in the number 452, the digit 2 is in the ones (or "units") place, the digit 5 is in the tens place, and the digit 4 is in the hundreds place. The name of each location corresponds to the "value" of that place. Thus:

2 is worth two "units" (two "ones"), or 2 (= 2 × 1).

5 is worth five tens, or 50 (= 5 × 10).

4 is worth four hundreds, or 400 (= 4 × 100).

We can now write the number 452 as the **sum** of these products:

452 = 4 × 100 + 5 × 10 + 2 × 1   ("four hundreds plus five tens plus two ones")

The chart to the left analyzes the place value of all the digits in the number:

692,567,891,023.8347

Notice that the place values to the left of the decimal all end in "-s," while the place values to the right of the decimal all end in "-ths." This is because the suffix "-ths" gives these places (to the right of the decimal) a fractional value.

6	9	2	5	6	7	8	9	1	0	2	3	.	8	3	4	7
HUNDRED	TEN	ONE	HUNDRED	TEN	ONE	HUNDRED	TEN		HUNDRED	TENS	UNITS OR		TENTHS	HUNDRED	THOUSAND	TEN
BILLIONS	BILLIONS	BILLIONS	MILLIONS	MILLIONS	MILLIONS	THOUSANDS	THOUSANDS	THOUSANDS			ONES			THS		THOUSANDTHS

Let us analyze the end of the preceding number: **0.8347**

8 is in the tenths place, giving it a value of 8 tenths, or $\dfrac{8}{10}$.

3 is in the hundredths place, giving it a value of 3 hundredths, or $\dfrac{3}{100}$.

4 is in the thousandths place, giving it a value of 4 thousandths, or $\dfrac{4}{1000}$.

7 is in the ten thousandths place, giving it a value of 7 ten thousandths, or $\dfrac{7}{10,000}$.

To use a concrete example, 0.8 might mean eight tenths of one dollar, which would be 8 dimes or 80 cents. Additionally, 0.03 might mean three hundredths of one dollar, which would be 3 pennies or 3 cents.

Check Your Skills

1. How many digits are in 99,999?
2. In the number 4,472.1023, in what place value is the "1"?

Answers can be found on page 59.

Adding Zeroes to Decimals

Adding zeroes to the end of a decimal or taking zeroes away from the end of a decimal does not change the value of the decimal. For example: 3.6 = 3.60 = 3.6000

Be careful, however, not to add or remove any zeroes from within a number. Doing so will change the value of the number: 7.01 ≠ 7.1

Powers of 10: Shifting the Decimal

Place values continually decrease from left to right by powers of 10. Understanding this can help you understand the following shortcuts for multiplication and division.

When you multiply any number by a positive power of ten, move the decimal forward (right) the specified number of places. This makes positive numbers larger:

$3.9742 \times 10^3 = 3,974.2$ (Move the decimal forward 3 spaces.)
$89.507 \times 10 = 895.07$ (Move the decimal forward 1 space.)

When you divide any number by a positive power of ten, move the decimal backward (left) the specified number of places. This makes positive numbers smaller:

$4,169.2 \div 10^2 = 41.692$ (Move the decimal backward 2 spaces.)
$89.507 \div 10 = 8.9507$ (Move the decimal backward 1 space.)

Note that if you need to add zeroes in order to shift a decimal, you should do so:

$2.57 \times 10^6 = 2,570,000$ (Add 4 zeroes at the end.)
$14.29 \div 10^5 = 0.0001429$ (Add 3 zeroes at the beginning.)

Finally, note that negative powers of ten reverse the regular process:

$6,782.01 \times 10^{-3} = 6.78201$ $53.0447 \div 10^{-2} = 5,304.47$

You can think about these processes as **trading decimal places for powers of ten**. Think about why this is. The expression 10^{-3} is equal to 0.001. If you multiply 6,782.01 by 0.001, you get a much smaller number.

For instance, all of the following numbers equal 110,700.

110.7	$\times$	10^3
11.07	$\times$	10^4
1.107	$\times$	10^5
0.1107	$\times$	10^6
0.01107	$\times$	10^7

The first number gets smaller by a factor of 10 as we move the decimal one place to the left, but the second number gets bigger by a factor of 10 to compensate.

Check Your Skills

3. $0.0652 \times 10^{-2} = ?$

4. $\dfrac{264}{10^{-6}} = ?$

5. Put these numbers in order from least to greatest:
    a. 234×10^{-2} b. 0.234×10^2 c. 2.34×10^4

Answers can be found on page 59.

*Manhattan*GRE*Prep

The Heavy Division Shortcut

Some division problems involving decimals can look rather complex. But sometimes, you only need to find an approximate solution. In these cases, you often can save yourself time by using the Heavy Division Shortcut: move the decimals in the same direction and round to whole numbers.

What is $1{,}530{,}794 \div (31.49 \times 10^4)$ to the nearest whole number?

Step 1: Set up the division problem in fraction form:

$$\frac{1{,}530{,}794}{31.49 \times 10^4}$$

Step 2: Rewrite the problem, eliminating powers of 10:

$$\frac{1{,}530{,}794}{314{,}900}$$

Step 3: Your goal is to get a single digit to the left of the decimal in the denominator. In this problem, you need to move the decimal point backward 5 spaces. You can do this to the denominator as long as you do the same thing to the numerator. (Technically, what you are doing is dividing top and bottom by the same power of 10: 100,000)

$$\frac{1{,}530{,}794}{314{,}900} = \frac{15.30794}{3.14900}$$

Now you have the single digit 3 to the left of the decimal in the denominator.

Step 4: Focus only on the whole number parts of the numerator and denominator and solve.

$$\frac{15.30794}{3.14900} \approx \frac{15}{3} = 5.$$

An approximate answer to this complex division problem is 5. If this answer is not precise enough, keep one more decimal place and do long division (eg., $153 \div 31 \approx 4.9$).

Check Your Skills

6. What is the integer closest to $\dfrac{64{,}239{,}028}{16{,}127{,}512}$?

Answers can be found on page 59.

Decimal Operations

ADDITION AND SUBTRACTION

To add or subtract decimals, make sure to line up the decimal points. Then add zeroes to make the right sides of the decimals the same length.

4.319 + 221.8   **10 − 0.063**

Line up the	4.319	Line up the	10.000
decimal points	+ 221.800	decimal points	− 0.063
and add zeroes.	226.119	and add zeroes.	9.937

Addition & Subtraction: Line up the decimal points!

<u>MULTIPLICATION</u>

To multiply decimals, ignore the decimal point until the end. Just multiply the numbers as you would if they were whole numbers. Then count the *total* number of digits to the right of the decimal point in the factors. The product should have the same number of digits to the right of the decimal point.

0.02 × 1.4   Multiply normally: 14
                                                 × 2
                                                 28

There are 3 digits to the right of the decimal point in the factors (0 and 2 in the first factor and 4 in the second factor). Therefore, move the decimal point 3 places to the left in the product: 28 → 0.028.

Multiplication: In the factors, count all the digits to the right of the decimal point—then put that many digits to the right of the decimal point in the product.

If the product ends with 0, count it in this process: 0.8 × 0.5 = 0.40, since 8 × 5 = 40.

If you are multiplying a very large number and a very small number, the following trick works to simplify the calculation: move the decimals **in the opposite direction** the same number of places.

   0.0003 × 40,000 = ?

   Move the decimal point RIGHT four places on the 0.0003 → 3
   Move the decimal point LEFT four places on the 40,000 → 4

   0.0003 × 40,000 = 3 × 4 = 12

The reason this technique works is that you are multiplying and then dividing by the same power of ten. In other words, you are **trading decimal places** in one number for decimal places in another number. This is just like trading decimal places for powers of ten, as we saw earlier.

<u>DIVISION</u>

If there is a decimal point in the dividend (the inner number) only, you can simply bring the decimal point straight up to the answer and divide normally.

Ex. **12.42 ÷ 3** = 4.14

$$
\begin{array}{r}
4.14 \\
3\overline{)12.42} \\
\underline{12} \\
04 \\
\underline{3} \\
12
\end{array}
$$

However, if there is a decimal point in the divisor (the outer number), you should shift the decimal point to the right in both the divisor and the dividend to make the *divisor* a whole number. Then, bring the decimal point up and divide. Be sure to shift the decimal in both numbers before dividing.

Ex: **12.42 ÷ 0.3** → 124.2 ÷ 3 = 41.4

$$
\begin{array}{r}
41.4 \\
3\overline{)124.2} \\
\underline{12} \\
04 \\
\underline{3} \\
12
\end{array}
$$

Move the decimal one space to the right to make 0.3 a whole number. Then, move the decimal one space in 12.42 to make it 124.2.

Division: Divide by whole numbers!

You can always simplify division problems that involve decimals by shifting the decimal point **in the same direction** in both the divisor and the dividend, even when the division problem is expressed as a fraction:

$$\frac{0.0045}{0.09} = \frac{45}{900}$$

Move the decimal 4 spaces to the right to make both the numerator and the denominator whole numbers.

Note that this is essentially the same process as simplifying a fraction. You are simply multiplying the numerator and denominator of the fraction by a power of ten—in this case, 10^4, or 10,000.

Keep track of how you move the decimal point! To simplify multiplication, you can move decimals in opposite directions. But to simplify division, you move decimals in the same direction.

Equivalently, by adding zeroes, you can express the numerator and the denominator as the same units, then simplify:

$$\frac{0.0045}{0.09} = \frac{0.0045}{0.0900} = 45 \text{ ten-thousandths} \div 900 \text{ ten-thousandths} = \frac{45}{900} = \frac{45}{900} = \frac{5}{100} = 0.05$$

Check Your Skills

7. $62.8 + 4.5768 = ?$
8. $7.125 - 4.309 = ?$
9. $0.00018 \times 600{,}000 = ?$
10. $85.702 \div 0.73 = ?$

Answers can be found on pages 59–60.

Check Your Skills Answer Key:

1. **5**: There are 5 digits in 99,999. Although there are only 9s, the 9 takes up 5 digits places (ten thousands, thousands, hundreds, tens and ones).

2. **Tenths place:** In the number 4, 472.1023, the 1 is in the tenths place.

3. **0.000652:** Move the decimal to the left when you multiply by 10 raised to a negative power. In this case move the decimal to the left two places.

$0.0652 \times 10^{-2} = 0.000652$

4. **264,000,000:** Move the decimal to the right when dividing by 10 raised to a negative power. In this case, move the decimal to the right 6 places.

$$\frac{264}{10^{-6}} = 264,000,000$$

5. **a, b, c:**

a = **2.34**
b = **23.4**
c = **23,400**

6. **4:** With large numbers, we can effectively ignore the smaller digits.

$$\frac{64,239,028}{16,127,512} \approx \frac{64,239,028}{16,127,512} \approx \frac{64}{16} \approx 4$$

7. **67.3768:**   62.8
              + 4.5768
              67.3768

8. **2.816:**   7.125
              − 4.309
              2.816

9. **108:** Trade decimal places. Change 0.00018 to 18 by moving the decimal to the right 5 places. To compensate, move the decimal of 600,000 to the left 5 places, making it 6. The multiplication problem is now:

$18 \times 6 = 108$

10. **117.4:** Be sure to move the decimal so that you are dividing by whole numbers with both the dividend and divisor. $85.702 \div 0.73 \rightarrow 8{,}570.2 \div 73$

$$
\begin{array}{r}
117.4 \\
73\overline{)8570.2} \\
\underline{73} \\
127 \\
\underline{73} \\
540 \\
\underline{511} \\
292 \\
\underline{292} \\
0
\end{array}
$$

Problem Set

Solve each problem, applying the concepts and rules you learned in this section.

1.   If k is an integer, and if 0.02468×10^k is greater than 10,000, what is the least possible value of k?

2.   Which integer values of b would give the number $2002 \div 10^{-b}$ a value between 1 and 100?

3.   Estimate to the nearest 10,000: $\dfrac{4,509,982,344}{5.342 \times 10^4}$

4.   Simplify: $(4.5 \times 2 + 6.6) \div 0.003$

5.   Simplify: $(4 \times 10^{-2}) - (2.5 \times 10^{-3})$

6.   What is $4,563,021 \div 10^5$, rounded to the nearest whole number?

7.   Simplify: $(0.08)^2 \div 0.4$

8.   Simplify: $[8 - (1.08 + 6.9)]^2$

9.   Which integer values of j would give the number $-37,129 \times 10^j$ a value between -100 and -1?

10.   Simplify: $\dfrac{0.00081}{0.09}$

11.

Column A	**Column B**
$\dfrac{573}{10^{-2}}$	0.573×10^5

12.

Column A	**Column B**
$\dfrac{603,789,420}{13.3 \times 10^7}$	5

13.

Column A	Column B
$\left(1+\dfrac{2}{5}\right) \cdot 0.25$	0.35

1. **6:** Multiplying 0.02468 by a positive power of ten will shift the decimal point to the right. Simply shift the decimal point to the right until the result is greater than 10,000. Keep track of how many times you shift the decimal point. Shifting the decimal point 5 times results in 2,468. This is still less than 10,000. Shifting one more place yields 24,680, which is greater than 10,000.

2. **{−2, −3}:** In order to give 2002 a value between 1 and 100, we must shift the decimal point to change the number to 2.002 or 20.02. This requires a shift of either two or three places to the left. Remember that, while multiplication shifts the decimal point to the right, division shifts it to the left. To shift the decimal point 2 places to the left, we would divide by 10^2. To shift it 3 places to the left, we would divide by 10^3. Therefore, the exponent $-b = \{2, 3\}$, and $b = \{-2, -3\}$.

3. **90,000:** Use the Heavy Division Shortcut to estimate:

$$\frac{4,509,982,344}{53,420} \approx \frac{4,500,000,000}{50,000} = \frac{450,000}{5} = 90,000$$

4. **5,200:** Use the order of operations, PEMDAS (Parentheses, Exponents, Multiplication & Division, Addition and Subtraction) to simplify. Remember that the numerator acts as a parentheses in a fraction.

$$\frac{9+6.6}{0.003} = \frac{15.6}{0.003} = \frac{15,600}{3} = 5,200$$

5. **0.0375:** First, rewrite the numbers in standard notation by shifting the decimal point. Then, add zeroes, line up the decimal points, and subtract.

$$\begin{array}{r} 0.0400 \\ - \ 0.0025 \\ \hline 0.0375 \end{array}$$

6. **46:** To divide by a positive power of 10, shift the decimal point to the left. This yields 45.63021. To round to the nearest whole number, look at the tenths place. The digit in the tenths place, 6, is more than five. Therefore, the number is closest to 46.

7. **0.016:** Use the order of operations, PEMDAS (Parentheses, Exponents, Multiplication & Division, Addition and Subtraction) to simplify. Shift the decimals in the numerator and denominator so that you are dividing by an integer.

$$\frac{(0.08)^2}{0.4} = \frac{0.0064}{0.4} = \frac{0.064}{4} = 0.016$$

8. **0.0004:** Use the order of operations, PEMDAS (Parentheses, Exponents, Multiplication & Division, Addition and Subtraction) to simplify.

First, add 1.08 + 6.9 by lining up the decimal points:

$$\begin{array}{r} 1.08 \\ + \ 6.9 \\ \hline 7.98 \end{array}$$

Then, subtract 7.98 from 8 by lining up the decimal points, adding zeroes to make the decimals the same length:

$$\begin{array}{r} 8.00 \\ -7.98 \\ \hline 0.02 \end{array}$$

Finally, square 0.02, conserving the number of digits to the right of the decimal point.

$$
\begin{array}{r}
0.02 \\
\times\ 0.02 \\
\hline
0.0004
\end{array}
$$

9. **{−3, −4}:** In order to give −37,129 a value between −100 and −1, we must shift the decimal point to change the number to −37.129 or −3.7129. This requires a shift of either two or three places to the left. Remember that multiplication shifts the decimal point to the right. To shift the decimal point 3 places to the left, we would multiply by 10^{-3}. To shift it 4 places to the left, we would multiply by 10^{-4}. Therefore, the exponent $j = \{-3, -4\}$.

10. **0.009:** Shift the decimal point 2 spaces to eliminate the decimal point in the denominator.

$$
\frac{0.00081}{0.09} = \frac{0.081}{9}
$$

Then divide. First, drop the 3 decimal places: $81 \div 9 = 9$. Then put the 3 decimal places back: 0.009

11. **C:** When you are dividing by 10 raised to a negative exponent, you move the decimal to the right. 573 becomes 57,300.

Column A	**Column B**
$\dfrac{573}{10^{-2}} =$	0.573×10^{5}
57,300	

When you are multiplying by 10 raised to a positive exponent, move the decimal to the right. 0.573 becomes 57,300

Column A	**Column B**
	$0.573 \times 10^{5} =$
57,300	**57,300**

12. **B:** Column A looks pretty intimidating. The trap here is to try to find an exact value for the expression in Column A. Let's estimate instead:

603,789,420 is about 600,000,000.

13.3×10^{7} is about 133,000,000, or even better 130,000,000

Column A	**Column B**
$\dfrac{603,789,420}{13.3 \times 10^7} \approx$	
	5
$\dfrac{600,000,000}{130,000,000}$	

Now you can cross off the zeros.

Column A	**Column B**
$\dfrac{60\cancel{0,000,000}}{13\cancel{0,000,000}} =$	
	5
$\dfrac{60}{13}$	

Multiply both columns by 13.

Column A	**Column B**
$\dfrac{60}{13} \times 13 =$	
	$5 \times 13 = \mathbf{65}$
60	

3. **C:** Whenever you want to multiply fractions or decimals, you should convert the numbers to fractions. Simplify the parentheses in Column A and convert 0.25 to a fraction.

Column A	**Column B**
$\left(1 + \dfrac{2}{5}\right) \cdot 0.25 =$	
$\left(\dfrac{5}{5} + \dfrac{2}{5}\right) \cdot \left(\dfrac{1}{4}\right) =$	0.35
$\left(\dfrac{7}{5}\right) \cdot \left(\dfrac{1}{4}\right) = \dfrac{\mathbf{7}}{\mathbf{20}}$	

Now compare 7/20 and 0.35. Put 0.35 into fraction form and reduce.

Column A	**Column B**
$\dfrac{7}{20}$	$0.35 =$
	$\dfrac{35}{100} = \dfrac{7}{\mathbf{20}}$

Chapter 3
of

FRACTIONS, DECIMALS, & PERCENTS

PERCENTS

In This Chapter . . .

- Percents as Fractions: The Percent Table
- Benchmark Values: 10% and 5%
- Percent Increase and Decrease
- Percent Change vs. Percent of Original
- Successive Percents
- Smart Numbers: Pick 100

PERCENTS

The other major way to express a part–whole relationship (in addition to decimals and fractions) is to use percents. Percent literally means "per one hundred." One can conceive of percent as simply a special type of fraction or decimal that involves the number 100.

> 75% of the students like chocolate ice cream.

This means that, out of every 100 students, 75 like chocolate ice cream. In fraction form, we write this as $\frac{75}{100}$, which simplifies to $\frac{3}{4}$.

In decimal form, we write this as 0.75 or seventy–five hundredths. Note that the last digit of the percent is in the hundredths place value.

One common mistake is the belief that 100% equals 100. This is not correct. In fact, 100% means $\frac{100}{100}$, or one hundred hundredths. Therefore, 100% = 1.

Percent problems occur frequently on the GRE. The key to these percent problems is to make them concrete by picking real numbers with which to work.

Percents as Fractions: The Percent Table

A simple but useful way of structuring basic percent problems on the GRE is by relating percents to fractions through a percent table as shown below.

A PART is some PERCENT of a WHOLE.

	Numbers	Percentage Fraction
PART		
WHOLE		100

$$\frac{\text{PART}}{\text{WHOLE}} = \frac{\text{PERCENT}}{100}$$

Example 1:   What is 30% of 80?

We are given the whole and the percent, and we are looking for the part. First, we fill in the percent table. Then we set up a proportion, cancel, cross–multiply, and solve:

	Numbers	Percentage Fraction
PART	x	30
WHOLE	80	100

$$\frac{x}{80} = \frac{3\cancel{0}}{10\cancel{0}} = \frac{3}{10} \qquad 10x = 240 \qquad x = 24$$

We can also solve this problem using decimal equivalents: $(0.30)(80) = (3)(8) = 24$

Example 2:   75% of what number is 21?

We are given the part and the percent, and we are looking for the whole. First, we fill in the percent table. Then we set up a proportion, cancel, cross–multiply, and solve:

PART	21	75
WHOLE	x	100

$\dfrac{21}{x} = \dfrac{\cancel{75}}{\cancel{100}} = \dfrac{3}{4}$ $3x = 84$ $x = 28$

Likewise, we can also solve this problem using decimal equivalents:

$(0.75)x = 21$ then move the decimal $\rightarrow$ $75x = 2{,}100$ $x = 28$

Example 3:   90 is what percent of 40?

We are given the part and the whole, and we are looking for the percent. Note that the "part" (90) is BIGGER than the "whole" (40). That is okay. Just make sure that you are taking the percent OF the "whole." Here, we are taking a percent OF 40, so 40 is the "whole."

First, we fill in the percent table. Then we set up a proportion again and solve:

PART	90	x
WHOLE	40	100

$\dfrac{\cancel{90}}{\cancel{40}} = \dfrac{9}{4} = \dfrac{x}{100}$ $4x = 900$ $x = 225$

90 is 225% of 40. Notice that you wind up with a percent BIGGER than 100%. That is what you should expect when the "part" is bigger than the "whole."

Check Your Skills

1. 84 is 70% of what number?
2. 30 is what percent of 50?

Answers can be found on page 77.

Benchmark Values: 10% and 5%

To find 10% of any number, just move the decimal point to the left one place.

10% of 500 is 50   10% of 34.99 = 3.499   10% of 0.978 is 0.0978

Once you know 10% of a number, it is easy to find 5% of that number: 5% is half of 10%.

10% of 300 is 30   5% of 300 is 30 ÷ 2 = 15

These quick ways of calculating 10% and 5% of a number can be useful for more complicated percentages.

What is 35% of 640?

Instead of multiplying 640 by 0.35, begin by finding 10% and 5% of 640.

10% of 640 is 64   5% of 640 is 64 ÷ 2 = 32

35% of a number is the same as (3 × 10% of a number) + (5% of a number).

3 × 64 + 32 = 192 + 32 = 224

You can also use the benchmark values to estimate percents. For example:

> Karen bought a new television, originally priced at $690. However, she had a coupon that saved her $67. For what percent discount was Karen's coupon?

You know that 10% of 690 would be 69. Therefore, 67 is slightly less than 10% of 690.

Check Your Skills

3. What is 10% of 145.028?
4. What is 20% of 73?

Answers can be found on page 77.

Percent Increase and Decrease

Some percent problems involve the concept of percent change. For example:

> The price of a cup of coffee increased from 80 cents to 84 cents. By what percent did the price change?

Percent change problems can be solved using our handy percent table, with a small adjustment. The price change (84 − 80 = 4 cents) is considered the part, while the ***original*** price (80 cents) is considered the whole.

CHANGE	4	x
ORIGINAL	80	100

$$\frac{\text{CHANGE}}{\text{ORIGINAL}} = \frac{\text{PERCENT}}{100}$$

$$\frac{\cancel{4}}{\cancel{80}} = \frac{1}{20} = \frac{x}{100} \qquad 20x = 100 \qquad x = 5 \quad \text{Thus, the price increased by 5\%.}$$

By the way, do not forget to divide by the original! The percent change is NOT 4%, which may be a wrong answer choice.

Alternatively, a question might be phrased as follows:

> If the price of a $30 shirt decreased by 20%, what was the final price of the shirt?

The whole is the original price of the shirt. The percent change is 20%. In order to find the answer, we must first find the part, which is the amount of the decrease:

CHANGE	x	20
ORIGINAL	30	100

$$\frac{x}{30} = \frac{\cancel{20}}{\cancel{100}} = \frac{1}{5} \qquad 5x = 30 \qquad x = 6$$

Therefore, the price of the shirt decreased by $6. The final price of the shirt was $30 − $6 = $24.

Check Your Skills

5. A GRE score (math + verbal) increased from 1250 to 1600. By what percent did the score increase?
6. 15% of the water in a full 30 gallon drum evaporated. How much water is left?

Answers can be found on page 77.

Percent Change vs. Percent of Original

Looking back at the cup of coffee problem, we see that the new price (84 cents) was higher than the original price (80 cents).

We can ask what percent OF the original price is represented by the new price.

$$\frac{\cancel{84}}{\cancel{80}} = \frac{21}{20} = \frac{x}{100} \qquad 20x = 2,100 \qquad x = 105$$

Thus, the new price is 105% OF the original price. Remember that the percent CHANGE is 5%. That is, the new price is 5% HIGHER THAN the original price. There is a fundamental relationship between these numbers, resulting from the simple idea that the CHANGE equals the NEW value minus the ORIGINAL value, or equivalently, ORIGINAL + CHANGE = NEW:

If a quantity is increased by *x* percent, then the new quantity is (100 + *x*)% OF the original. Thus a 15% increase produces a quantity that is 115% OF the original.

We can write this relationship thus: $\text{ORIGINAL} \times \left(1 + \frac{\text{Percent Increase}}{100} \right) = \text{NEW}$

In the case of the cup of coffee, we see that $80 \times \left(1 + \frac{5}{100} \right) = 80(1.05) = 84$.

Likewise, in the shirt problem, we had a 20% decrease in the price of a $30 shirt, resulting in a new price of $24.

The new price is some percent OF the old price. Let us calculate that percent.

$$\frac{\cancel{24}}{\cancel{30}} = \frac{4}{5} = \frac{x}{100} \qquad 5x = 400 \qquad x = 80$$

Thus, the new price (20% LESS THAN the original price) is 80% OF the original price.

If a quantity is decreased by *x* percent, then the new quantity is (100 − *x*)% OF the original. Thus a 15% decrease produces a quantity that is 85% OF the original.

We can write this relationship thus: $\text{ORIGINAL} \times \left(1 - \frac{\text{Percent Decrease}}{100} \right) = \text{NEW}$.

In the case of the shirt, we see that $30 \times \left(1 - \frac{20}{100} \right) = 30(0.80) = 24$.

These formulas are all just another way of saying ORIGINAL ± CHANGE = NEW.

Example 4:   What number is 50% greater than 60?

The whole is the original value, which is 60. The percent change (i.e., the percent "greater than") is 50%. In order to find the answer, we must first find the part, which is the amount of the increase:

CHANGE	x	50
ORIGINAL	60	100

$$\frac{x}{60} = \frac{50}{100} = \frac{1}{2} \qquad 2x = 60 \qquad x = 30$$

We know that ORIGINAL ± CHANGE = NEW. Therefore, the number that is 50% greater than 60 is 60 + 30 = 90, which is 150% of 60.

We could also solve this problem using the formula : $\text{ORIGINAL} \times \left(1 + \dfrac{\text{Percent Increase}}{100}\right) = \text{NEW}$

$$60\left(1 + \frac{50}{100}\right) = 60(1.5) = 90$$

Example 5:   What number is 150% greater than 60?

The whole is the original value, which is 60. The percent change (i.e., the percent "greater than") is 150%. In order to find the answer, we must first find the part, which is the amount of the increase:

CHANGE	x	150
ORIGINAL	60	100

$$\frac{x}{60} = \frac{150}{100} = \frac{3}{2} \qquad 2x = 180 \qquad x = 90$$

Now, x is the CHANGE, NOT the new value! **It is easy to forget to add back the original amount when the percent change is more than 100%.** Thus, the number that is 150% greater than 60 is 60 + 90 = 150, which is 250% of 60.

We could also solve this problem using the formula : $\text{ORIGINAL} \times \left(1 + \dfrac{\text{Percent Increase}}{100}\right) = \text{NEW}$

$$60\left(1 + \frac{150}{100}\right) = 60(2.5) = 150$$

Check Your Skills

7. A plant originally cost $35. The price is increased by 20%. The new price is what?
8. 70 is 250% greater than what number?

Answers can be found on page 77–78.

Successive Percents

One of the GRE's favorite tricks involves successive percents.

> If a ticket increased in price by 20%, and then increased again by 5%, by what percent did the ticket price increase in total?

Although it may seem counterintuitive, the answer is NOT 25%.

To understand why, consider a concrete example. Let us say that the ticket initially cost $100. After increasing by 20%, the ticket price went up to $120 ($20 is 20% of $100).

Here is where it gets tricky. The ticket price goes up again by 5%. However, it increases by 5% of the **NEW PRICE** of $120 (not 5% of the *original* $100 price). 5% of $120 is 0.05(120) = $6. Therefore, the final price of the ticket is $120 + $6 = $126.

You can now see that two successive percent increases, the first of 20% and the second of 5%, DO NOT result in a combined 25% increase. In fact, they result in a combined 26% increase (because the ticket price increased from $100 to $126).

Successive percents CANNOT simply be added together! This holds for successive increases, successive decreases, and for combinations of increases and decreases. If a ticket goes up in price by 30% and then goes down by 10%, the price has NOT in fact gone up a net of 20%. Likewise, if an index increases by 15% and then falls by 15%, it does NOT return to its original value! (Try it—you will see that the index is down 2.25% overall.)

A great way to solve successive percent problems is to choose real numbers and see what happens. The preceding example used the real value of $100 for the initial price of the ticket, making it easy to see exactly what happened to the ticket price with each increase. **Usually, 100 will be the easiest real number to choose for percent problems.**

You could also solve by converting to decimals. Increasing a price by 20% is the same as multiplying the price by 1.20.

Increasing the new price by 5% is the same as multiplying that new price by 1.05.

Thus, you can also write the relationship this way:

$$\text{ORIGINAL} \times (1.20) \times (1.05) = \text{FINAL PRICE}$$

When you multiply 1.20 by 1.05, you get 1.26, indicating that the price increased by 26% overall.

This approach works well for problems that involve many successive steps (e.g., compound interest). However, in the end, it is still usually best to pick $100 for the original price and solve using concrete numbers.

Check Your Skills

9. If your stock portfolio increased by 25% and then decreased by 20%, what percent of the original would your new stock portfolio be?

Answers can be found on page 78.

Smart Numbers: Pick 100

Sometimes, percent problems on the GRE include unspecified numerical amounts; often these unspecified amounts are described by variables.

> A shirt that initially cost *d* dollars was on sale for 20% off. If *s* represents the sale price of the shirt, *d* is what percentage of *s*?

This is an easy problem that might look confusing. To solve percent problems such as this one, simply pick 100 for the unspecified amount (just as we did when solving successive percents).

If the shirt initially cost $100, then *d* = 100. If the shirt was on sale for 20% off, then the new price of the shirt is $80. Thus, *s* = 80.

The question asks: *d* is what percentage of *s*, or 100 is what percentage of 80? Using a percent table, we fill in 80 as the whole and 100 as the part (even though the part happens to be larger than the whole in this case). We are looking for the percent, so we set up a proportion, cross–multiply, and solve:

PART	100	*x*
WHOLE	80	100

$$\frac{100}{80} = \frac{x}{100} \qquad 80x = 10,000 \qquad x = 125$$

Therefore, *d* is 125% of *s*.

The important point here is that, like successive percent problems and other percent problems that include unspecified amounts, this example is most easily solved by plugging in a real value. For percent problems, the easiest value to plug in is generally 100. **The fastest way to success with GRE percent problems with unspecified amounts is to pick 100 as a value.**

Check Your Skills

10. If your stock portfolio decreased by 25% and then increased by 20%, what percent of the original would your new stock portfolio be?

Answers can be found on page 78.

Check Your Skills Answer Key

1. **120:**

PART	84	70
WHOLE	x	100

$$\frac{84}{x} = \frac{70}{100} = \frac{7}{10} \qquad 7x = 840 \qquad x = 120$$

2. **60:**

PART	30	x
WHOLE	50	100

$$\frac{x}{100} = \frac{30}{50} = \frac{3}{5} \qquad 5x = 300 \qquad x = 60$$

3. **14.5028:** Move the decimal to the left one place. 145.028 $\rightarrow$ 14.5028

4. **14.6:** To find 20% of 73, first find 10% of 73. Move the decimal to the left one place. 73 $\rightarrow$ 7.3. 20% is twice 10%.

$$7.3 \times 2 = 14.6$$

5. **28%:** First find the change: 1600 − 1250 = 350.

$$\frac{\text{CHANGE}}{\text{ORIGINAL}} = \frac{350}{1250} = \frac{7}{25} = \frac{7 \times 4}{25 \times 4} = \frac{28}{100} = 28\%$$

6. **4.5:**

CHANGE	x	15
ORIGINAL	30	100

$$\frac{x}{30} = \frac{15}{100} = \frac{3}{20} \qquad 20x = 90 \qquad x = 4.5$$

7. **42:** Recall that $\text{ORIGINAL} \times \left(1 + \dfrac{\text{Percent Increase}}{100}\right) = \text{NEW}$.

$$35 \times \left(1 + \frac{20}{100}\right) = 35(1.2) = 42$$

8. **20:** Recall that $\text{ORIGINAL} \times \left(1 + \dfrac{\text{Percent Increase}}{100}\right) = \text{NEW}$. Designate the original value x.

$$x \times \left(1 + \frac{250}{100}\right) = 70$$
$$3.5x = 70$$
$$x = 20$$

9. **100%:** Pick 100 for the original value of the portfolio. A 25% increase equals

$100(1.25) = 125$

A 20% decrease equals

$125(0.8) = 100$

The final value is 100. Because the starting value was also 100, the portfolio is 100% of its original value.

10. **90%:** Pick 100 for the original value of the portfolio. A 25% decrease equals

$100(0.75) = 75$

A 20% increase equals

$75(1.2) = 90$

The final value is 90 and the original value was 100. $\dfrac{90}{100} = 90\%$ of the original value.

Problem Set

Solve the following problems. Use a percent table to organize percent problems, and pick 100 when dealing with unspecified amounts.

1. x% of y is 10. y% of 120 is 48. What is x?

2.   A stereo was marked down by 30% and sold for $84. What was the presale price of the stereo?

3.   From 1980 to 1990, the population of Mitannia increased by 6%. From 1991 to 2000, it decreased by 3%. What was the overall percentage change in the population of Mitannia from 1980 to 2000?

4.   If y is decreased by 20% and then increased by 60%, what is the new number, expressed in terms of y?

5.   A 7% car loan, which is compounded annually, has an interest payment of $210 after the first year. What is the principal on the loan?

6.   A bowl was half full of water. 4 cups of water were then added to the bowl, filling the bowl to 70% of its capacity. How many cups of water are now in the bowl?

7.   A large tub is filled with 920 units of alcohol and 1,800 units of water. 40% of the water evaporates. What percent of the remaining liquid is water?

8. x is 40% of y. 50% of y is 40. 16 is what percent of x?

9.   800, increased by 50% and then decreased by 30%, yields what number?

10.   If 1,600 is increased by 20%, and then reduced by y%, yielding 1,536, what is y?

11.

Steve uses a certain copy
machine that reduces an
image by 13%

Column A   **Column B**

The percent of the original if Steve   75%
reduces the image by another 13%

12.

y is 50% of x% of x

<u>Column A</u>	<u>Column B</u>
y	x

13.

<u>Column A</u>	<u>Column B</u>
10% of 643.38	20% of 321.69

1. **25:** We can use two percent tables to solve this problem. Begin with the fact that $y\%$ of 120 is 48:

PART	48	y
WHOLE	120	100

$4,800 = 120y$
$y = 40$

Then, set up a percent table for the fact that $x\%$ of 40 is 10.

PART	10	x
WHOLE	40	100

$1,000 = 40x$
$x = 25$

We can also set up equations with decimal equivalents to solve:

$(0.01y)(120) = 48$, so $1.2y = 48$ or $y = 40$. Therefore, since we know that $(0.01x)(y) = 10$, we have:

$$(0.01x)(40) = 10 \qquad 40x = 1,000 \qquad x = 25$$

2. **$120:** We can use a percent table to solve this problem. Remember that the stereo was marked down 30% from the original, so we have to solve for the original price.

CHANGE	x	30
ORIGINAL	$\$84 + x$	100

$\dfrac{x}{84 + x} = \dfrac{30}{100}$ $100x = 30(84 + x)$ $100x = 30(84) + 30x$

$70x = 30(84)$ $x = 36$

Therefore, the original price was $(84 + 36) = \$120$.

We could also solve this problem using the formula : $\text{ORIGINAL} \times \left(1 - \dfrac{\text{Percent Decrease}}{100}\right) = \text{NEW}$

$$x\left(1 - \dfrac{30}{100}\right) = 84 \qquad 0.7x = 84 \qquad x = 120$$

3. **2.82% increase:** For percent problems, the Smart Number is 100. Therefore, assume that the population of Mitannia in 1980 was 100. Then, apply the successive percents to find the overall percent change:

     From 1980–1990, there was a 6% increase: $100(1 + 0.06) = 100(1.06) = 106$
     From 1991–2000, there was a 3% decrease: $106(1 - 0.03) = 106(0.97) = 102.82$
     Overall, the population increased from 100 to 102.82, representing a 2.82% increase.

4. **1.28y:** For percent problems, the Smart Number is 100. Therefore, assign y a value of 100. Then, apply the successive percent to find the overall percentage change:

     (1) y is decreased by 20%: $100(1 - 0.20) = 100(0.8) = 80$
     (2) Then, it is increased by 60%: $80(1 + 0.60) = 80(1.6) = 128$
     Overall, there was a 28% increase. If the original value of y is 100, the new value is $1.28y$.

5. **$3,000:** We can use a percent table to solve this problem, which helps us find the decimal equivalent equation.

PART	210	7
WHOLE	x	100

$21,000 = 7x$
$x = 3,000$

6. 14: There are some problems for which you cannot use Smart Numbers, since the total amount can be calculated. This is one of those problems. Instead, use a percent table:

PART	$0.5x + 4$	70
WHOLE	x	100

$$\frac{0.5x+4}{x} = \frac{70}{100} = \frac{7}{10} \qquad \begin{array}{c} 5x + 40 = 7x \\ 40 = 2x \end{array} \qquad x = 20$$

The capacity of the bowl is 20 cups. There are 14 cups in the bowl {70% of 20, or 0.5(20) + 4}.

PART	4	20
WHOLE	x	100

Alternately, the 4 cups added to the bowl represent 20% of the total capacity. Use a percent table to solve for x, the whole. Since $x = 20$, there are 14 (50% of 20 + 4) cups in the bowl.

7. 54%: For this liquid mixture problem, set up a table with two columns: one for the original mixture and one for the mixture after the water evaporates from the tub.

	Original	After Evaporation
Alcohol	920	920
Water	1,800	$0.60(1,800) = 1,080$
TOTAL	2,720	2,000

The remaining liquid in the tub is $\dfrac{1,080}{2,000}$, or 54%, water.

We could also solve for the new amount of water using the formula:

$$\text{ORIGINAL} \times \left(1 - \frac{\text{Percent Decrease}}{100} \right) = \text{NEW}$$

$$1,800 \left(1 - \frac{40}{100} \right) = (1,800)(0.6) = 1,080 \text{ units of water. Water is } \frac{1,080}{920 + 1,080} = \frac{1,080}{2,000} = 54\% \text{ of the total.}$$

8. 50%: Use two percent tables to solve this problem. Begin with the fact that 50% of y is 40:

PART	40	50
WHOLE	y	100

$$\begin{array}{c} 4,000 = 50y \\ y = 80 \end{array}$$

Then, set up a percent table for the fact that x is 40% of y.

PART	x	40
WHOLE	80	100

$$\begin{array}{c} 3,200 = 100x \\ x = 32 \end{array}$$

Finally, 16 is 50% of 32. We could alternatively set up equations with decimal equivalents to solve: $x = (0.4)y$ We also know that $(0.5)y = 40$, so $y = 80$ and $x = (0.4)(80) = 32$. Therefore, 16 is half, or 50%, of x.

9. 840: Apply the successive percent to find the overall percentage change:
    (1) 800 is increased by 50%: $800 \times 1.5 = 1,200$
    (2) Then, the result is decreased by 30%: $1,200 \times 0.7 = 840$

10. **20:** Apply the percents in succession with two percent tables.

$$192,000 = 100x$$
$$x = 1,920$$

PART	x	120
WHOLE	1,600	100

Then, fill in the "change" for the part (1,920 − 1,536 = 384) and the original for the whole (1,920).

$$1,920y = 38,400$$
$$y = 20$$

PART	384	y
WHOLE	1,920	100

Alternatively we could solve for the new number using formulas. Because this is a successive percents problem, we need to "chain" the formula: once to reflect the initial increase in the number, then twice to reflect the subsequent decrease:

$$\text{ORIGINAL} \times \left(1 + \frac{\text{Percent Increase}}{100}\right) \times \left(1 - \frac{\text{Percent Decrease}}{100}\right) = \text{NEW}$$

$$1,600 \times \left(1 + \frac{20}{100}\right) \times \left(1 - \frac{y}{100}\right) = 1,536 \qquad 1,920 \times \left(1 - \frac{y}{100}\right) = 1,536 \qquad 1,920 - \frac{1,920\,y}{100} = 1,536$$

$$1,920 - 1,536 = 19.2\,y \qquad\qquad 384 = 19.2\,y \qquad\qquad 20 = y$$

11. **A:** In dealing with percents problems, we should choose 100. In this case, the original size of the image is 100. The question tells us that Steve reduces the image by 13%.

$$100 - 0.13(100) = 100 - 13 = 87$$

So our image is at 87. Column A tells us that we have to reduce the image size by another 13%.

If the image size is reduced by 13%, then 87% of the image remains. Multiply 87 (the current size of the image) by 0.87 (87% expressed as a decimal).

$$87 \times 0.87 = 75.69$$

Steve uses a certain copy
machine that reduces an image
by 13%

Column A	Column B
The percent of the original if Steve reduces the image by another 13% = **75.69%**	75%

12. **D:** First translate the statement in the common information into an equation.

$$y = 0.5 \times \frac{x}{100} \times x$$

$$y = \frac{x^2}{200}$$

$$200y = x^2$$

Now try to pick some easy numbers. If $y = 1$, then $x = \sqrt{200}$, which is definitely bigger than 1.

y is 50% of x% of x

Column A	**Column B**
$y = 1$	$x = \sqrt{200}$

However, if $y = 200$, then x must also equal 200.

y is 50% of x% of x

Column A	**Column B**
$y = 200$	$x = 200$

y can be less than x, but y can also be equal to x. The correct answer is D.

13. **C:** To calculate 10% of 643.38, move the decimal to the left one place. 643.38 → 64.338

Column A	**Column B**
10% of 643.38 = **64.338**	20% of 321.69

To calculate 20% of 321.69, don't multiply by 0.2. Instead, find 10% first by moving the decimal to the left one place. 321.69 → 32.169

Now multiply by 2: 32.169 × 2 = 64.338

Column A	**Column B**
64.338	20% of 321.69 = **64.338**

Chapter 4
of
FRACTIONS, DECIMALS, & PERCENTS

FDP
CONNECTIONS

In This Chapter . . .

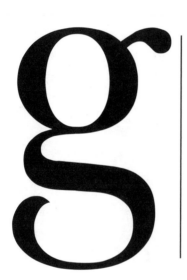

- Converting FDPs
- Converting Among Fractions, Decimals, and Percents
- Common FDP Equivalents
- When To Use Which Form
- FDPs and Word Translations
- FDP Word Problems

FDP CONNECTIONS

In This Chapter:

- The common thread between fractions, decimals, and percents
- How to convert numbers in one form to another form (e.g., changing percents to decimals)
- How to use fractions, decimals, and percents to solve certain types of GRE word problems

Fractions, Decimals, and Percents: Three Ways to Say the Same Thing!

Fractions, decimals, and percents are three different ways of representing the same thing: "parts of a whole."

Consider the following:

1/3 of the orange   *2.5 times the distance*   *110% of the sales*

In each of these instances, we're using a fraction, a decimal, or a percent to indicate that we have some portion of a whole. In fact, these different forms are very closely related. For instance, we might say that a container is 1/2 full, which is the same thing as saying that it is 50% full, or filled to 0.5 of its capacity. To illustrate, see the table below. Each row consists of a fraction, a decimal, and a percent representing the same part of a whole.

Fraction	Decimal	Percent
$\frac{1}{4}$ ¼ 1/4	0.25	25%
The container is 1/2 full.	The container is filled to 0.5 of its capacity.	The container is 50% full.
3/2	1.5	150%

Thus, one helpful feature of fractions, decimals, and percents is that we can use whichever form is most convenient to solve a particular problem. We've already discussed fractions, decimals and percents individually. This chapter is devoted to changing from one form to another so that you can choose the form best suited to answering the question at hand,

Converting FDPs

From Percent to Decimal or Fraction

Percent to Decimal

As we discussed earlier, to convert from a percent to a decimal, simply move the decimal point two spots to the left.

53% becomes 0.53

40.57% becomes 0.4057

3% becomes 0.03

Percent to Fraction

To convert from a percent to a fraction, remember that *per cent* literally means "per hundred," so put the percent over one hundred and then simplify.

45% becomes 45/100 = 9/20

8% becomes 8/100 = 2/25

Check Your Skills

1. Change 87% to a decimal.
2. Change 30% to a fraction.

Answers can be found on page 97.

From Decimal to Percent or Fraction

Decimal to Percent

To convert from a decimal to a percent, simply move the decimal point two spots to the right.

0.53 becomes 53%

0.4057 becomes 40.57%

0.03 becomes 3%

Decimal to Fraction

To convert from decimal to fraction, it helps to remember the proper names for the digits—the first digit to the right of the decimal point is the tenths digit, next is the hundredth digit, and then the thousandth digit, and so on.

4	5	7	.	1	2	3	5
Hundreds	Tens	Units		Tenths	Hundredths	Thousandths	Ten Thousandths

The number of zeroes in the denominator should match the number of digits in the decimal (besides the 0 in front of the decimal point). For example:

0.3 is three tenths, or 3/10

0.23 is twenty-three hundredths, or 23/100

0.007 is seven thousandths, or 7/1000

Check Your Skills

3. Change 0.37 to a percent.
4. Change 0.25 to a fraction.

Answers can be found on page 97.

From Fraction to Decimal or Percent

Fraction to Decimal

To convert from a fraction to a decimal, long-divide the numerator by the denominator:

$$3/8 \text{ is } 3 \div 8 = 0.375$$

$$\begin{array}{r} 0.375 \\ 8\overline{)3.000} \end{array}$$

$$1/4 \text{ is } 1 \div 4 = 0.25$$

$$\begin{array}{r} 0.25 \\ 4\overline{)1.00} \end{array}$$

Fraction to Percent

To convert from a fraction to a percent, first convert from fraction to decimal, and then convert that decimal to a percent.

Step 1: $1/2 = 1 \div 2 = 0.50$

Step 2: $0.50 = 50\%$

Dividing the numerator by the denominator can be cumbersome and time consuming. Ideally, you should have the most basic conversions memorized before test day. A list of common FDP conversions appear later in the chapter that you should memorize.

Check Your Skills

5. Change 3/5 to a decimal.
6. Change 3/8 to a percent.

Answers can be found on page 97.

Converting Among Fractions, Decimals, and Percents

The following chart reviews the ways to convert from fractions to decimals, from decimals to fractions, from fractions to percents, from percents to fractions, from decimals to percents, and from percents to decimals. You should practice so that each becomes natural to you.

TO → / FROM ↓	FRACTION $\frac{3}{8}$	DECIMAL 0.375	PERCENT 37.5%
FRACTION $\frac{3}{8}$		Divide the numerator by the denominator: $3 \div 8 = 0.375$ Use long division if necessary.	Divide the numerator by the denominator and move the decimal two places to the right: $3 \div 8 = 0.375 \rightarrow 37.5\%$
DECIMAL 0.375	Use the place value of the last digit in the decimal as the denominator, and put the decimal's digits in the numerator. Then simplify: $\frac{375}{1000} = \frac{3}{8}$		Move the decimal point two places to the right: $0.375 \rightarrow 37.5\%$
PERCENT 37.5%	Use the digits of the percent for the numerator and 100 for the denominator. Then simplify: $\frac{37.5}{100} = \frac{3}{8}$	Find the percent's decimal point and move it two places to the left: $37.5\% \rightarrow 0.375$	

Common FDP Equivalents

You should memorize the following common equivalents:

Fraction	Decimal	Percent
$\frac{1}{100}$	0.01	1%
$\frac{1}{50}$	0.02	2%
$\frac{1}{25}$	0.04	4%
$\frac{1}{20}$	0.05	5%
$\frac{1}{10}$	0.10	10%
$\frac{1}{9}$	$0.\overline{11} \approx 0.111$	$\approx 11.1\%$
$\frac{1}{8}$	0.125	12.5%
$\frac{1}{6}$	$0.1\overline{6} \approx 0.167$	$\approx 16.7\%$
$\frac{1}{5}$	0.2	20%
$\frac{1}{4}$	0.25	25%
$\frac{3}{10}$	0.3	30%
$\frac{1}{3}$	$0.\overline{3} \approx 0.333$	$\approx 33.3\%$
$\frac{3}{8}$	0.375	37.5%
$\frac{2}{5}$	0.4	40%
$\frac{1}{2}$	0.5	50%

Fraction	Decimal	Percent
$\frac{3}{5}$	0.6	60%
$\frac{5}{8}$	0.625	62.5%
$\frac{2}{3}$	$0.\overline{6} \approx 0.667$	$\approx 66.7\%$
$\frac{7}{10}$	0.7	70%
$\frac{3}{4}$	0.75	75%
$\frac{4}{5}$	0.8	80%
$\frac{5}{6}$	$0.8\overline{3} \approx 0.833$	$\approx 83.3\%$
$\frac{7}{8}$	0.875	87.5%
$\frac{9}{10}$	0.9	90%
$\frac{1}{1}$	1	100%
$\frac{5}{4}$	1.25	125%
$\frac{4}{3}$	$1.\overline{3} \approx 1.33$	133%
$\frac{3}{2}$	1.5	150%
$\frac{7}{4}$	1.75	175%

When To Use Which Form

Fractions are good for cancelling factors in multiplications. They are also the best way of exactly expressing proportions that do not have clean decimal equivalents, such as 1/7. Switch to fractions if there is a handy fractional equivalent of the decimal or percent and/or you think you can cancel lots of factors.

> What is 37.5% of 240?

If you simply convert the percent to a decimal and multiply, you will have to do a fair bit of arithmetic:

$$\begin{array}{r} 0.375 \\ \times\,240 \\ \hline 0 \\ 15000 \\ 75000 \\ \hline 90.000 \end{array}$$

Alternatively, you can recognize that $0.375 = \dfrac{3}{8}$.

So we have $(0.375)(240) = \left(\dfrac{3}{\cancel{8}}\right)\left(\cancel{240}^{\,30}\right) = 3(30) = 90$.

This is much faster!

> A dress is marked up $16\dfrac{2}{3}\%$ to a final price of $140. What is the original price of the dress?

From the previous page, we know that $16\dfrac{2}{3}\%$ is equivalent to $\dfrac{1}{6}$. Thus, adding $\dfrac{1}{6}$ of a number to itself is the same thing as multiplying by $1 + \dfrac{1}{6} = \dfrac{7}{6}$:

$$\frac{7}{6}x = 140 \qquad x = \left(\frac{6}{7}\right)140 = \left(\frac{6}{\cancel{7}}\right)\cancel{140}^{\,20} = 120\,.\ \text{The original price is \$120.}$$

Decimals, on the other hand, are good for estimating results or for comparing sizes. The reason is that the basis of comparison is equivalent (there is no denominator). The same holds true for **percents**. The implied denominator is always 100, so you can easily compare percents (of the same whole) to each other.

To convert certain fractions to decimals or percents, multiply top and bottom by the same number:

$$\frac{17}{25} = \frac{17 \times 4}{25 \times 4} = \frac{68}{100} = 0.68 = 68\%$$

This process is faster than long division, but it only works when the denominator has only 2's and/or 5's as factors.

In some cases, you might find it easier to compare a bunch of fractions by giving them all a common denominator, rather than by converting them all to decimals or percents. The general rule is this: **prefer fractions for doing multiplication or division, but prefer decimals and percents for doing addition or subtraction, for estimating numbers, or for comparing numbers.**

FDPs and Word Translations

Fractions, decimals, and percents show up in many Word Translation problems. Make sure that you understand and can apply the very common translations below.

In the Problem	Translation

<u>In the Problem</u>   <u>Translation</u>

X percent

$$\dfrac{X}{100}$$

of   Multiply

of Z Z is the Whole

Y is X percent of Z Y is the Part, and Z is the Whole

$$Y = \left(\dfrac{X}{100}\right)Z$$

$$\text{Part} = \left(\dfrac{\text{Percent}}{100}\right) \times \text{Whole}$$

Y is X percent of Z Alternative: $\dfrac{Y}{Z} = \dfrac{X}{100}$

$$\dfrac{\text{Part}}{\text{Whole}} = \dfrac{\text{Percent}}{100}$$

A is $\dfrac{1}{6}$ of B $A = \left(\dfrac{1}{6}\right)B$

C is 20% of D $C = (0.20)D$

E is 10% greater than F $E = (1.10)F$

G is 30% less than H $G = (100\% - 30\%)H = (0.70)H$

The dress cost $\$J$.
Then it was marked up 25% $\text{Profit} = \text{Revenue} - \text{Cost}$
and sold.

What is the profit? $\text{Profit} = (1.25)J - J$
                                    $\text{Profit} = (0.25)J$

FDP Word Problems

As we mentioned earlier, the purpose of fractions, decimals, and percents is to represent the proportions between a part and a whole.

Most FDP Word Problems hinge on these fundamental relationships:

$$\text{Part} = \text{Fraction} \times \text{Whole}$$

$$\text{Part} = \text{Decimal} \times \text{Whole}$$

In general, these problems will give you two parts of the equation and ask you to figure out the third.

Let's look at three examples:

> A quarter of the students attended the pep rally. If there are a total of 200 students, how many of them attended the pep rally?

In this case, we are told the fraction and the total number of students. We are asked to find the number of students who attended the pep rally.

$$a = (1/4)(200)$$
$$a = 50$$

Fifty students attended the pep rally.

> At a certain pet shop, there are four kittens, two turtles, eight puppies, and six snakes. If there are no other pets, what percentage of the store's animals are kittens?

Here we are told the part (there are four kittens) and the whole (there are $4 + 2 + 8 + 6 = 20$ animals total). We are asked to find the percentage.

$$4 = x(20)$$
$$4 \div 20 = x$$
$$0.2 = x$$

To answer the question, we convert the decimal 0.2 to 20%. Twenty percent of the animals are kittens.

> Sally receives a commission equal to thirty percent of her sales. If Sally earned $4,500 in commission last month, what were her total sales?

Here we are given the part, and told what percent that part is, but we don't know the whole. We are asked to solve for the whole.

$$4{,}500 = 0.30s$$
$$4{,}500 \div 0.30 = s$$
$$s = 15{,}000$$

Her total sales for the month were $15,000.

Tip: If in doubt—sound it out! Do you ever get confused on how exactly to set up an equation for a word problem? If so, you're not alone! For instance, consider the following problem:

   x is forty percent of what number?

First, let's assign a variable to the number we're looking for—let's call it *y*.

Do we set this up as 40% × *x* = (*y*), or *x* = 40% (*y*)?

If you are unsure of how to set up this equation, try this—say it aloud or to yourself. Often, that will clear up any confusion, and put you on the right track.

Let's illustrate, using our two options.

	Equation	**Read out loud as...**
Option 1:	40% × *x* = (*y*)	40% of *x* = *y*
Option 2:	*x* = 40% (*y*)	*x* is 40% of *y*

Now, it's much easier to see that the second option, *x* = 40% (*y*), is the equation that represents our original question.

Check Your Skills

Write the following sentences as equations.

7. *x* is 60% of *y*.
8. 1/3 of *a* is *b*.
9. *y* is 25% of what number?

Answers can be found on pages 97.

Typical Complications

Now let's take those three problems and give them a little GRE twist.

   "A quarter of the students attended the pep rally. If there are a total of 200 students, how many of them did not attend the pep rally?"

Notice here that the fraction we are given, a quarter, represents the students who did attend the pep rally, but we are asked to find the number that did *not* attend the pep rally.

Here are two ways we can solve this:

1. Find the value of one quarter and subtract from the whole.

   $a = (1/4)(200)$
   $a = 50$

Once we figure out 50 students did attend, we can see that 200 − 50 = 150, so 150 did not attend.

OR

2. Find the value of the remaining portion.

If 1/4 did attend, that must mean 3/4 did not attend:

$$n = (3/4)(200)$$
$$n = 150$$

> "At a certain pet shop, there are four kittens, two turtles, eight puppies, and six snakes. If there are no other pets, what percentage of the store's animals do kittens and puppies represent?"

Here we are asked to combine two different elements. We can take either of two approaches.

1. Figure each percentage out separately and then add.

$$4 = x(20)$$
$$0.2 = x$$

$$8 = y(20)$$
$$0.4 = y$$

$$0.2 + 0.4 = 0.6$$

Kittens and puppies represent 60% of the animals.

OR

2. Add the quantities first and then solve.

There are four kittens and eight puppies, for a total of $4 + 8 = 12$ of these animals:

$$12 = x(20)$$
$$0.6 = x$$

Kittens and puppies represent 60% of the animals.

> "Sally receives a monthly salary of $1,000 plus 30% of her total sales. If Sally earned $5,500 last month, what were her total sales?"

In this case, a constant ($1,000) has been added in to the proportion equation.

Her salary = $1,000 + 0.30(total sales)

$$5,500 = 1000 + 0.3(s)$$
$$4,500 = 0.3(s)$$
$$15,000 = s$$

Check Your Skills

10. A water drum is filled to 1/4 of its capacity. If another 30 gallons of water were added, the drum would be filled. How many gallons of water does the drum currently contain?

The answer can be found on page 97.

Check Your Skills Answer Key

1. **0.87:** Change 87% to a decimal.
   87% becomes 0.87

2. **3/10:** Change 30% to a fraction.
   30% becomes 30/100, which reduces to 3/10

3. **37%:** Change 0.37 to a percent.
   0.37 becomes 37%

4. **1/4:** Change 0.25 to a fraction.
   0.25 is 25 hundredths, so it becomes 25/100, which reduces to 1/4

5. **0.6:** Change 3/5 to a decimal.
   3/5 is $3 \div 5 = 0.6$

6. **37.5%:** Change 3/8 to a percent.
   Step 1: 3/8 is $3 \div 8 = 0.375$
   Step 2: $0.375 = 37.5\%$

7. $x = 60\%\ (y)$
   $x = 0.6(y)$

8. $1/3$ of a is b.
   $(1/3)a = b$

9. y is 25% of what number?
   Let x = the number in question.
   $y = 25\%\ (x)$
   $y = 0.25(x)$

10. **10 gallons:** A water drum is filled to 1/4 of its capacity. If another 30 gallons of water were added, the drum would be filled. How many gallons of water does the drum currently contain?

Let x be the capacity of the water drum. If the drum is 1/4 full, and 30 gallons would make it full, then
$30 = (1 - 1/4)x$, which means:

$$30 = \frac{3}{4}x$$

Divide both sides by 3/4. This is equivalent to multiplying by 4/3.

$$30 = \frac{3}{4}x$$

$$\frac{4}{3} \times 30 = x$$

$$\frac{4}{\cancel{3}} \times \cancel{30}\,10 = x$$

$$40 = x$$

If the total capacity is 40 gallons and the drum is 1/4 full, then the drum currently contains $1/4 \times 40 = 10$ gallons.

Problem Set

1. Express the following as fractions: 2.45 0.008

2. Express the following as fractions: 420% 8%

3. Express the following as decimals: $\dfrac{9}{2}$ $\dfrac{3{,}000}{10{,}000}$

4. Express the following as decimals: $1\dfrac{27}{4}$ $12\dfrac{8}{3}$

5. Express the following as percents: $\dfrac{1{,}000}{10}$ $\dfrac{25}{9}$

6. Express the following as percents: 80.4 0.0007

7. Order from least to greatest: $\dfrac{8}{18}$ 0.8 40%

8. Order from least to greatest: 1.19 $\dfrac{120}{84}$ 131.44%

9. Order from least to greatest: $2\dfrac{4}{7}$ 2400% 2.401

10. Order from least to greatest ($x \neq 0$): $\dfrac{50}{17}x^2$ $2.9x^2$ $(x^2)(3.10\%)$

11. Order from least to greatest: $\dfrac{500}{199}$ 248,000% 2.9002003

12. What number is 62.5% of 192?

13. 200 is 16% of what number?

For problems #14–15, express your answer in terms of the variables given (X, Y, and possibly Z).

14. What number is X percent of Y?

15. X is what percent of Y?

16.

For every 1,000,000 toys sold,
337,000 are action figures

Column A		Column B
Percent of toys sold that are action figures		33.7%

17.

Column A		Column B
$10^{-3} \cdot \left(\dfrac{0.002}{10^{-3}} \right)$		0.02

18.

$1,600 worth of $20 bills are
stacked up and reach 32
inches high.

Column A		Column B
$1,050 worth of $10 bills are stacked up (assume all denominations are the same height). The percent that the height of the stack of $10 bills is greater than the height of the stack of $20 bills		33.5%

1. To convert a decimal to a fraction, write it over the appropriate power of ten and simplify.

$$2.45 = 2\frac{45}{100} = 2\frac{9}{20} \text{ (mixed)} = \frac{49}{20} \text{ (improper)}$$

$$0.008 = \frac{8}{1,000} = \frac{1}{125}$$

2. To convert a percent to a fraction, write it over a denominator of 100 and simplify.

$$420\% = \frac{420}{100} = \frac{1}{125} \text{ (improper)} = 4\frac{1}{125} \text{ (mixed)}$$

$$8\% = \frac{8}{100} = \frac{2}{25}$$

3. To convert a fraction to a decimal, divide the numerator by the denominator.

$$\frac{9}{2} = 9 \div 2 = 4.5$$

It often helps to simplify the fraction BEFORE you divide:

$$\frac{3,000}{10,000} = \frac{3}{10} = 0.3$$

4. To convert a mixed number to a decimal, simplify the mixed number first, if needed.

$$1\frac{27}{4} = 1 + 6\frac{3}{4} = 7\frac{3}{4}$$

$$12\frac{8}{3} = 12 + 2\frac{2}{3} = 14.\overline{6}$$

Note: you do not have to know the "repeating bar" notation, but you should know that 2/3 = 0.6666...

5. To convert a fraction to a percent, rewrite the fraction with a denominator of 100.

$$\frac{1,000}{10} = \frac{10,000}{100} = 10,000\%$$

Or convert the fraction to a decimal and shift the decimal point two places to the right.

$$\frac{25}{9} = 25 \div 9 = 2.7777\ldots = 2.\overline{7} = 277.\overline{7}\%$$

6. To convert a decimal to a percent, shift the decimal point two places to the right.
   80.4 = **8,040%**
   0.0007 = **0.07%**

7. $40\% < \dfrac{8}{18} < 0.8$: To order from least to greatest, express all the terms in the same form.

$$\frac{8}{18} = \frac{4}{9} = 0.4444\ldots = 0.\overline{4}$$
$$0.8 = 0.8$$
$$40\% = 0.4$$
$$0.4 < 0.\overline{4} < 0.8$$

Alternately, you can use FDP logic and Benchmark Values to solve this problem: $\dfrac{8}{18}$ is $\dfrac{1}{18}$ less than $\dfrac{1}{2}$. 40% is 10% (or $\dfrac{1}{10}$) less than $\dfrac{1}{2}$. Since $\dfrac{8}{18}$ is a smaller piece away from $\dfrac{1}{2}$, it is closer to $\dfrac{1}{2}$ and therefore larger than 40%. 0.8 is clearly greater than $\dfrac{1}{2}$. Therefore, $40\% < \dfrac{8}{18} < 0.8$.

8. $1.19 < 131.44\% < \dfrac{120}{84}$: To order from least to greatest, express all the terms in the same form.

$$1.19 = 1.19$$
$$\frac{120}{84} \approx 1.4286$$
$$131.44\% = 1.3144$$
$$1.19 < 1.3144 < 1.4286$$

9. $2.401 < 2\dfrac{4}{7} < 2400\%$: To order from least to greatest, express all the terms in the same form.

$$2\frac{4}{7} \approx 2.57$$
$$2{,}400\% = 24$$
$$2.401 = 2.401$$

Alternately, you can use FDP logic and Benchmark Values to solve this problem: 2400% is 24, which is clearly the largest value. Then, use Benchmark Values to compare $2\dfrac{4}{7}$ and 2.401. Since the whole number portion, 2, is the same, just compare the fraction parts. $\dfrac{4}{7}$ is greater than $\dfrac{1}{2}$. 0.401 is less than $\dfrac{1}{2}$. Therefore, $2\dfrac{4}{7}$ must be greater than 2.401. So, $2.401 < 2\dfrac{4}{7} < 2{,}400\%$.

10. $3.10\% < 2.9 < \dfrac{50}{17}$: To order from least to greatest, express all the terms in the same form.

(Note that, since x^2 is a positive term common to all the terms you are comparing, you can ignore its presence completely. If the common term were negative, then the order would be reversed.)

*Manhattan*GRE* Prep
the new standard

$$\frac{50}{17} = 2\frac{16}{17} \approx 2.94$$ 　　　(You can find the first few digits of the decimal by long division.)

$$2.9 = 2.9$$
$$3.10\% = 0.0310$$
$$0.0310 < 2.9 < 2.94$$

Alternately, you can use FDP logic and Benchmark Values to solve this problem: 3.10% is 0.0310, which is clearly the smallest value. Then, compare 2.9 and $2\frac{16}{17}$ to see which one is closer to 3. 2.9 is $\frac{1}{10}$ away from 3. $2\frac{16}{17}$ is $\frac{1}{17}$ away from 3. Since $\frac{1}{17}$ is smaller than $\frac{1}{10}$, $2\frac{16}{17}$ is closest to 3; therefore, it is larger. So,

$$3.10\% < 2.9 < \frac{50}{17}.$$

11. $\mathbf{\dfrac{500}{199}} < \mathbf{2.9002003} < \mathbf{248,000\%}$: To order from least to greatest, express all the terms in the same form.

$$\frac{500}{199} \approx 2.51$$ 　　　(You can find the first few digits of the decimal by long division.)
$$248,000\% = 2,480$$
$$2.9002003 = 2.9002003$$

Alternately, you can use FDP logic and Benchmark Values to solve this problem: 248,000% = 2,480, which is clearly the largest value. $\frac{500}{199}$ is approximately $\frac{500}{200}$, or $\frac{5}{2}$, which is 2.5. This is clearly less than 2.9002003. Therefore, $\frac{500}{199} < 2.9002003 < 248,000\%$.

12. **120:** This is a percent vs. decimal conversion problem. If you simply recognize that $62.5\% = 0.625 = \frac{5}{8}$, this problem will be a lot easier: $\frac{5}{8} \times 192 = \frac{5}{1} \times 24 = 120$. Multiplying 0.625×240 will take much longer to complete.

13. **1,250:** This is a percent vs. decimal conversion problem. If you simply recognize that $16\% = 0.16 = \frac{16}{100} = \frac{4}{25}$, this problem will be a lot easier: $\frac{4}{25}x = 200$, so $x = 200 \times \frac{25}{4} = 50 \times 25 = 1,250$. Dividing out $200 \div 0.16$ will probably take longer to complete.

14. $\dfrac{XY}{100}$: We can use decimal equivalents. X percent is $\dfrac{X}{100}$, and we simply need to multiply by Y.

Alternatively we can set up a table and solve for the unknown (in this case, we will call it Z):

PART	Z	X
WHOLE	Y	100

$100Z = XY$

$Z = \dfrac{XY}{100}$

15. $\dfrac{100X}{Y}$: We can use decimal equivalents. X equals some unknown percent of Y (call it Z percent), so

$X = \dfrac{Z}{100} \times Y$, and we simply solve for Z: $\dfrac{100X}{Y} = Z$.

Alternatively we can set up a table and solve for the unknown Z:

PART	X	Z
WHOLE	Y	100

$100X = ZY$

$Z = \dfrac{100X}{Y}$

16. **C:** Simplify Column A. We can divide the number of action figures by the total number of toys to find the percentage of action figures.

For every 1,000,000 toys sold,
337,000 are action figures

Column A	**Column B**
Percent of toys sold that are action figures =	33.7%
$\dfrac{337,000}{1,000,000}$	

A percentage is defined as being out of 100, so reduce the fraction until the denominator is 100.

Column A	**Column B**
$\dfrac{337,000}{1,000,000} = \dfrac{337,\cancel{0}\,\cancel{0}\,\cancel{0}}{1,000,\cancel{0}\,\cancel{0}\,\cancel{0}} =$	33.7%
$\dfrac{337}{1,000} = \dfrac{\mathbf{33.7}}{\mathbf{100}}$	

Because the denominator is 100, the number in the numerator is the percent. So action figures are 33.7% of the total number of toys.

17. **B:** Take a close look at the expression in Column A. 0.002 is first divided by 10^{-3}, and then multiplied by 10^{-3}. The net effect is the same as multiplying by 1. The two 10^{-3}'s cancel out.

<table>
<tr><td align="center">**Column A**</td><td align="center">**Column B**</td></tr>
<tr><td align="center">$10^{-3} \cdot \left(\dfrac{0.002}{10^{-3}} \right) =$</td><td align="center">0.02</td></tr>
<tr><td align="center">$0.002 \cdot \dfrac{10^{-3}}{10^{-3}} =$</td><td></td></tr>
<tr><td align="center">$0.002 \cdot 1 = \mathbf{0.002}$</td><td></td></tr>
</table>

18. **B:** Because all bills have the same height, we can compare the number of bills in each stack directly to determine the percent increase in height. The number of $20 bills in a stack with a value of $1,600 is

$$1600/20 = 80$$

The number of $10 bills in a stack with a value of $1,050 is

$$1,050/10 = 105$$

Plug these values into the percent change formula to evaluate Column A.

$1,600 worth of $20 bills
are stacked up and reach
32 inches high.

Column A	**Column B**
$1,050 worth of $10 bills are stacked up (assume all denominations are the same height). The percent that the height of the stack of $10 bills is greater than the height of the stack of $20 bills =	33.5%

$$\frac{105 - 80}{80} = \frac{25}{80} = \frac{\mathbf{5}}{\mathbf{16}}$$

Now compare the two columns. $\dfrac{5}{16} < \dfrac{5}{15}$, so Column A must be less than $\dfrac{1}{3}$. Recall that $\dfrac{1}{3}$ is $33.\overline{3}\%$ as a

percent, so 33.5% is is slightly larger than $\dfrac{1}{3}$. Therefore the value in Column A must be less than 33.5%.

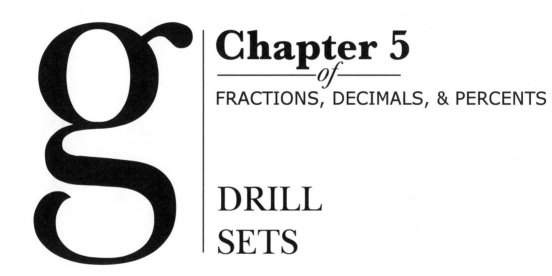

Chapter 5
of

FRACTIONS, DECIMALS, & PERCENTS

DRILL
SETS

In This Chapter . . .

- FDPs Drill Sets

DRILL SET 1:

Drill 1: For each of the following pairs of fractions, decide which fraction is larger

1. $\dfrac{1}{4}, \dfrac{3}{4}$

2. $\dfrac{1}{5}, \dfrac{1}{6}$

3. $\dfrac{53}{52}, \dfrac{85}{86}$

4. $\dfrac{7}{9}, \dfrac{6}{10}$

5. $\dfrac{700}{360}, \dfrac{590}{290}$

Drill 2: Add or subtract the following fractions.

1. $\dfrac{2}{7} + \dfrac{3}{7} =$

2. $\dfrac{5}{8} - \dfrac{4}{8} =$

3. $\dfrac{7}{9} - \dfrac{2}{9} =$

4. $\dfrac{9}{11} + \dfrac{20}{11} =$

5. $\dfrac{3}{4} - \dfrac{10}{4} =$

Drill 3: Add or subtract the following fractions.

1. $\dfrac{2}{3} + \dfrac{5}{9}$

2. $\dfrac{7}{8} - \dfrac{5}{4}$

3. $\dfrac{4}{9} + \dfrac{8}{11}$

4. $\dfrac{20}{12} - \dfrac{5}{3}$

5. $\dfrac{1}{4} + \dfrac{4}{5} + \dfrac{5}{8}$

DRILL 4: Solve for x in the following equations.

1. $\dfrac{1}{5} + \dfrac{x}{5} = \dfrac{4}{5}$

2. $\dfrac{x}{8} - \dfrac{3}{8} = \dfrac{10}{8}$

3. $\dfrac{x}{6} + \dfrac{5}{12} = \dfrac{11}{12}$

4. $\dfrac{2}{7} - \dfrac{x}{21} = -\dfrac{2}{21}$

5. $\dfrac{2}{5} + \dfrac{x}{8} = \dfrac{31}{40}$

DRILL SET 2:

Drill 1: Simplify the following fractions.

1. $\dfrac{6}{9}$

2. $\dfrac{12}{28}$

3. $\dfrac{24}{36}$

4. $\dfrac{35}{100}$

5. $\dfrac{6x}{70}$

Drill 2: Multiply or Divide the following fractions. Final answer must be simplified.

1. $\dfrac{4}{7} \times \dfrac{8}{9}$

2. $\dfrac{9}{4} \div \dfrac{2}{3}$

3. $\dfrac{7}{15} \div \dfrac{8}{5}$

4. $\dfrac{5}{12} \times \dfrac{8}{10}$

5. $\dfrac{3x}{13} \times \dfrac{5}{6}$

Drill 3: Multiply or Divide the following fractions. Final answer must be simplified.

1. $\dfrac{14}{20} \times \dfrac{15}{21}$

2. $\dfrac{6}{25} \div \dfrac{9}{10}$

3. $\dfrac{4}{21} \times \dfrac{14}{13} \times \dfrac{5}{8}$

4. $\dfrac{3}{11} \div \dfrac{3}{11}$

5. $\dfrac{57}{63} \times \dfrac{0}{18}$

Drill 4: Solve for x in the following equations.

1. $\dfrac{5}{3}x = \dfrac{3}{7}$

2. $\dfrac{2}{x} = \dfrac{7}{3}$

3. $\dfrac{6}{11}x = \dfrac{10}{33}$

4. $\dfrac{2x}{13} = \dfrac{3}{7}$

5. $\dfrac{3x}{4} - \dfrac{5}{6} = \dfrac{17}{12}$

DRILL SET 3:

DRILL 1: Convert the following improper fractions to mixed numbers.

1. $\dfrac{9}{4}$

2. $\dfrac{31}{7}$

3. $\dfrac{47}{15}$

4. $\dfrac{70}{20}$

5. $\dfrac{91}{13}$

Drill 2: Convert the following mixed numbers to improper fractions.

1. $3\frac{2}{3}$

2. $2\frac{1}{6}$

3. $6\frac{3}{7}$

4. $4\frac{5}{9}$

5. $12\frac{5}{12}$

DRILL SET 4:

DRILL 1: Evaluate the following expressions.

1. $6.75 \times 10^3 =$
2. $72.12 \times 10^{-4} =$
3. $2,346 \times 10^{-3} =$
4. $27.048 \times 10^2 =$
5. $54.197 / 10^2 =$

DRILL 2: Evaluate the following expressions.

1. $1 + 0.2 + 0.03 + 0.004 =$
2. $0.48 + 0.02 =$
3. $1.21 + 0.38 =$
4. $-0.02 + 0.35 =$
5. $0.370 + 0.042 =$

DRILL 3: Evaluate the following expressions.

1. $0.27 \times 2 =$
2. $0.403 \times 3 =$
3. $0.2 \times 0.2 =$
4. $20 \times 0.85 =$
5. $0.04 \times 0.201 =$

DRILL 4: Evaluate the following expressions.

1. $2.1 \times 0.08 =$
2. $0.063 \times 0.40 =$
3. $0.03 \times 0.005 =$
4. $0.75 (80) + 0.50 (20) =$
5. $100 \times 0.01 \times 0.01 =$

DRILL 5: Evaluate the following expressions.

1. $4/0.2 =$
2. $12.6/0.3 =$
3. $3.20/0.04 =$
4. $0.49/0.07 =$
5. $6/0.5 =$

DRILL SET 5:

DRILL 1: Fill in the missing information in the chart below:

Fraction	Decimal	Percent
1/100	0.01	1%
1/20		
	0.1	
1/8		
	0.2	
		25%
	0.3	
		33.33...%
3/8		
		40%
1/2		
	0.6	
		66.66...%
		70%
	0.75	
4/5	0.8	80%
	0.875	
9/10		
		100%

DRILL 2:

1. Convert 45% to a decimal.
2. Convert 70% to a fraction.
3. Convert 13.25% to a decimal.
4. Convert 36% to a fraction.
5. Convert 0.02% to a decimal.

DRILL 3:

1. Convert 0.20 to a percent.
2. Convert 0.55 to a fraction.
3. Convert 0.304 to a percent.
4. Convert 0.455 to a fraction.
5. Convert 0.375 to a fraction.

DRILL 4:

1. Convert 4/5 to a percent.
2. Convert 3/6 to a percent.
3. Convert 9/12 to a percent.
4. Convert 6/20 to a percent.
5. Convert 3/2 to a percent.

DRILL SET 6:

DRILL 1

1. Forty percent of the balls in a bag are red. If there is a total of 300 balls in the bag, how many of them are red?

2. Sally always puts 15% of her salary in a retirement fund. If she put $6,000 in her retirement fund last year, what was her salary?

3. Sixteen students wear glasses. If there are forty students total, what fraction of the students wear glasses?

4. What is the new price of an eighty-dollar sweater that has been discounted 20%?

5. Billy has twenty dollars and Johnny has thirty dollars. If both Billy and Johnny invest 25% of their money in baseball cards, how much money will they invest?

DRILL 2

1. Last year, a furniture store sold four hundred chairs, two hundred tables, four hundred couches, and nothing else. The chairs made up what percent of the total items sold?

2. At her old job, Sally earned a yearly salary of $80,000. At her new job, Sally earns a salary equal to $40,000 plus a commission of 25% on all her sales. If Sally wants to make a yearly salary at her new job that is the same as that of her old job, how much does she have to produce in terms of yearly sales?

3. Of 250 people surveyed, 36% said they preferred regular soda, 40% said they preferred diet soda, and the rest did not have a preference. How many of the 250 people did not have a preference?

4. A jar contains 1/3 red marbles and 1/2 blue marbles. The remaining 25 marbles are white. How many marbles does the jar contain?

5. Ted has 2/3 as many friends as Billy has, and Chris has 1/2 as many friends as Billy has. The number of friends Chris has is what percent of the number of friends Ted has?

Drill Set Answers

Set 1, Drill 1

1. $\dfrac{1}{4}, \dfrac{\mathbf{3}}{\mathbf{4}}$ – The denominators are the same, but the numerator of $\dfrac{3}{4}$ is larger, so $\dfrac{3}{4} > \dfrac{1}{4}$.

2. $\dfrac{\mathbf{1}}{\mathbf{5}}, \dfrac{1}{6}$ – The numerators are the same, but the denominator of $\dfrac{1}{5}$ is smaller, so $\dfrac{1}{5} > \dfrac{1}{6}$.

3. $\dfrac{\mathbf{53}}{\mathbf{52}}, \dfrac{85}{86}$ – In the first fraction, $\dfrac{53}{52}$, the numerator is bigger than the denominator, so the fraction is greater than 1. In the second fraction, $\dfrac{85}{86}$, the denominator is bigger than the numerator, so the fraction is less than 1. $\dfrac{53}{52} > \dfrac{85}{86}$.

4. $\dfrac{\mathbf{7}}{\mathbf{9}}, \dfrac{6}{10}$ – The second fraction, $\dfrac{6}{10}$, has both a smaller numerator and a larger denominator than the first fraction. Therefore, $\dfrac{6}{10} < \dfrac{7}{9}$.

5. $\dfrac{700}{360}, \dfrac{\mathbf{590}}{\mathbf{290}}$ – The first fraction is greater than 1 but less than 2, because 700 is less than twice 360 ($2 \times 360 = 720$). The second fraction is greater than 2, because 590 is more than twice 290 ($2 \times 290 = 580$). $\dfrac{590}{290} > \dfrac{700}{360}$.

Set 1, Drill 2

1. $\dfrac{\mathbf{5}}{\mathbf{7}}:$ $\dfrac{2}{7} + \dfrac{3}{7} = \dfrac{2+3}{7} = \dfrac{5}{7}$

2. $\dfrac{\mathbf{1}}{\mathbf{8}}:$ $\dfrac{5}{8} - \dfrac{4}{8} = \dfrac{5-4}{8} = \dfrac{1}{8}$

3. $\dfrac{\mathbf{5}}{\mathbf{9}}:$ $\dfrac{7}{9} - \dfrac{2}{9} = \dfrac{7-2}{9} = \dfrac{5}{9}$

4. $\dfrac{\mathbf{29}}{\mathbf{11}}:$ $\dfrac{9}{11} + \dfrac{20}{11} = \dfrac{9+20}{11} = \dfrac{29}{11}$

5. $\dfrac{\mathbf{-7}}{\mathbf{4}}:$ $\dfrac{3}{4} - \dfrac{10}{4} = \dfrac{3-10}{4} = \dfrac{-7}{4}$

Set 1, Drill 3

1. $\dfrac{11}{9}$: $\dfrac{2}{3}+\dfrac{5}{9}=\dfrac{2}{3}\times\dfrac{3}{3}+\dfrac{5}{9}=\dfrac{2\times3}{3\times3}+\dfrac{5}{9}=\dfrac{6}{9}+\dfrac{5}{9}=\dfrac{6+5}{9}=\dfrac{11}{9}$

2. $\dfrac{-3}{8}$: $\dfrac{7}{8}-\dfrac{5}{4}=\dfrac{7}{8}-\dfrac{5}{4}\times\dfrac{2}{2}=\dfrac{7}{8}-\dfrac{5\times2}{4\times2}=\dfrac{7}{8}-\dfrac{10}{8}=\dfrac{7-10}{8}=\dfrac{-3}{8}$

3. $\dfrac{116}{99}$: $\dfrac{4}{9}+\dfrac{8}{11}=\dfrac{4}{9}\times\dfrac{11}{11}+\dfrac{8}{11}\times\dfrac{9}{9}=\dfrac{4\times11}{9\times11}+\dfrac{8\times9}{11\times9}=\dfrac{44}{99}+\dfrac{72}{99}=\dfrac{116}{99}$

4. 0 : $\dfrac{20}{12}-\dfrac{5}{3}=\dfrac{20}{12}-\dfrac{5}{3}\times\dfrac{4}{4}=\dfrac{20}{12}-\dfrac{5\times4}{3\times4}=\dfrac{20}{12}-\dfrac{20}{12}=0$

5. $\dfrac{67}{40}$: $\dfrac{1}{4}+\dfrac{4}{5}+\dfrac{5}{8}=\dfrac{1}{4}\times\dfrac{10}{10}+\dfrac{4}{5}\times\dfrac{8}{8}+\dfrac{5}{8}\times\dfrac{5}{5}=\dfrac{1\times10}{4\times10}+\dfrac{4\times8}{5\times8}+\dfrac{5\times5}{8\times5}=$

$\dfrac{10}{40}+\dfrac{32}{40}+\dfrac{25}{40}=\dfrac{10+32+25}{40}=\dfrac{67}{40}$

Set 1, Drill 4

1. **3** : $\dfrac{1}{5}+\dfrac{x}{5}=\dfrac{4}{5}$

$\dfrac{x}{5}=\dfrac{4}{5}-\dfrac{1}{5}$

$\dfrac{x}{5}=\dfrac{4-1}{5}=\dfrac{3}{5}$

$x=3$

2. **13** : $\dfrac{x}{8}-\dfrac{3}{8}=\dfrac{10}{8}$

$\dfrac{x}{8}=\dfrac{10}{8}+\dfrac{3}{8}$

$\dfrac{x}{8}=\dfrac{10+3}{8}=\dfrac{13}{8}$

$x=13$

3. **3** : $\dfrac{x}{6}+\dfrac{5}{12}=\dfrac{11}{12}$

$\dfrac{x}{6}=\dfrac{11}{12}-\dfrac{5}{12}$

$\dfrac{x}{6}=\dfrac{11-5}{12}=\dfrac{6}{12}$

$\dfrac{x\times2}{6\times2}=\dfrac{2x}{12}=\dfrac{6}{12}$

$2x=6$

$x=3$

4. **8** : $\dfrac{2}{7}-\dfrac{x}{21}=-\dfrac{2}{21}$

$-\dfrac{x}{21}=-\dfrac{2}{21}-\dfrac{2}{7}$

$-\dfrac{x}{21}=-\dfrac{2}{21}-\dfrac{2\times3}{7\times3}$

$-\dfrac{x}{21}=-\dfrac{2}{21}-\dfrac{6}{21}=\dfrac{-2-6}{21}=\dfrac{-8}{21}$

$\dfrac{x}{21}=\dfrac{8}{21}$

$x=8$

*Manhattan*GRE*Prep

the new standard

5. **3 :** $\dfrac{2}{5}+\dfrac{x}{8}=\dfrac{31}{40}$

$\dfrac{x}{8}=\dfrac{31}{40}-\dfrac{2}{5}$

$\dfrac{x}{8}=\dfrac{31}{40}-\dfrac{2\times 8}{5\times 8}$

$\dfrac{x}{8}=\dfrac{31}{40}-\dfrac{16}{40}$

$\dfrac{x}{8}=\dfrac{15}{40}$

$\dfrac{x\times 5}{8\times 5}=\dfrac{5x}{40}=\dfrac{15}{40}$

$5x=15$

$x=3$

Set 2, Drill 1

1. $\dfrac{2}{3}$ **:** $\dfrac{6}{9}=\dfrac{2\times 3}{3\times 3}=\dfrac{2}{3}\times\dfrac{3}{3}=\dfrac{2}{3}$

2. $\dfrac{3}{7}$ **:** $\dfrac{12}{28}=\dfrac{2\times 2\times 3}{2\times 2\times 7}=\dfrac{3}{7}\times\dfrac{2\times 2}{2\times 2}=\dfrac{3}{7}$

3. $\dfrac{2}{3}$ **:** $\dfrac{24}{36}=\dfrac{2\times 2\times 2\times 3}{2\times 2\times 3\times 3}=\dfrac{2}{3}\times\dfrac{2\times 2\times 3}{2\times 2\times 3}=\dfrac{2}{3}$

4. $\dfrac{7}{20}$ **:** $\dfrac{35}{100}=\dfrac{5\times 7}{2\times 2\times 5\times 5}=\dfrac{7}{2\times 2\times 5}\times\dfrac{5}{5}=\dfrac{7}{20}$

5. $\dfrac{3x}{35}$ **:** $\dfrac{6x}{70}=\dfrac{2\times 3\times x}{2\times 5\times 7}=\dfrac{3\times x}{5\times 7}\times\dfrac{2}{2}=\dfrac{3x}{35}$

Set 2, Drill 2

1. $\dfrac{32}{63}$ **:** $\dfrac{4}{7}\times\dfrac{8}{9}=\dfrac{4\times 8}{7\times 9}=\dfrac{32}{63}$

2. $\dfrac{27}{8}$ **:** $\dfrac{9}{4}\div\dfrac{2}{3}=\dfrac{9}{4}\times\dfrac{3}{2}=\dfrac{9\times 3}{4\times 2}=\dfrac{27}{8}$

3. $\dfrac{7}{24}$ **:** $\dfrac{7}{15}\div\dfrac{8}{5}=\dfrac{7}{15}\times\dfrac{5}{8}=\dfrac{7\times 5}{3\times 5\times 8}=\dfrac{7\times \cancel{5}}{3\times \cancel{5}\times 8}=\dfrac{7}{24}$

4. $\dfrac{1}{3}$ **:** $\dfrac{5}{12}\times\dfrac{8}{10}=\dfrac{5\times 2\times 2\times 2}{2\times 2\times 3\times 2\times 5}=\dfrac{\cancel{5}\times\cancel{2}\times\cancel{2}\times\cancel{2}}{\cancel{2}\times\cancel{2}\times 3\times\cancel{2}\times\cancel{5}}=\dfrac{1}{3}$

5. $\dfrac{5x}{26}$ **:** $\dfrac{3x}{13}\times\dfrac{5}{6}=\dfrac{3\times x\times 5}{13\times 2\times 3}=\dfrac{\cancel{3}\times x\times 5}{13\times 2\times\cancel{3}}=\dfrac{5x}{26}$

Set 2, Drill 3

1. $\dfrac{\mathbf{1}}{\mathbf{2}}$: $\dfrac{14}{20} \times \dfrac{15}{21} = \dfrac{2 \times 7 \times 3 \times 5}{2 \times 2 \times 5 \times 7 \times 3} = \dfrac{\cancel{2} \times \cancel{7} \times \cancel{3} \times \cancel{5}}{2 \times \cancel{2} \times \cancel{5} \times \cancel{7} \times \cancel{3}} = \dfrac{1}{2}$

2. $\dfrac{\mathbf{4}}{\mathbf{15}}$: $\dfrac{6}{25} \div \dfrac{9}{10} = \dfrac{6}{25} \times \dfrac{10}{9} = \dfrac{2 \times 3 \times 2 \times 5}{5 \times 5 \times 3 \times 3} = \dfrac{2 \times \cancel{3} \times 2 \times \cancel{5}}{5 \times \cancel{5} \times \cancel{3} \times 3} = \dfrac{4}{15}$

3. $\dfrac{\mathbf{5}}{\mathbf{39}}$: $\dfrac{4}{21} \times \dfrac{14}{13} \times \dfrac{5}{8} = \dfrac{2 \times 2 \times 2 \times 7 \times 5}{3 \times 7 \times 13 \times 2 \times 2 \times 2} = \dfrac{\cancel{2} \times \cancel{2} \times \cancel{2} \times \cancel{7} \times 5}{3 \times \cancel{7} \times 13 \times \cancel{2} \times \cancel{2} \times \cancel{2}} = \dfrac{5}{39}$

4. **1** : $\dfrac{3}{11} \div \dfrac{3}{11} = \dfrac{3}{11} \times \dfrac{11}{3} = \dfrac{3 \times 11}{11 \times 3} = \dfrac{33}{33} = 1$

5. **0** : $\dfrac{57}{63} \times \dfrac{0}{18} = \dfrac{57 \times 0}{63 \times 18} = 0$

Set 2, Drill 4

1. $\dfrac{\mathbf{9}}{\mathbf{35}}$: $\dfrac{5}{3}x = \dfrac{3}{7}$

$x = \dfrac{3}{7} \div \dfrac{5}{3} = \dfrac{3}{7} \times \dfrac{3}{5}$

$x = \dfrac{9}{35}$

2. $\dfrac{\mathbf{6}}{\mathbf{7}}$: $\dfrac{2}{x} = \dfrac{7}{3}$

$2 \times 3 = 7 \times x$

$6 = 7x$

$\dfrac{6}{7} = x$

3. $\dfrac{\mathbf{5}}{\mathbf{9}}$: $\dfrac{6}{11}x = \dfrac{10}{33}$

$x = \dfrac{10}{33} \div \dfrac{6}{11} = \dfrac{10}{33} \times \dfrac{11}{6}$

$x = \dfrac{2 \times 5 \times 11}{3 \times 11 \times 2 \times 3} = \dfrac{\cancel{2} \times 5 \times \cancel{11}}{3 \times \cancel{11} \times \cancel{2} \times 3}$

$x = \dfrac{5}{9}$

4. $\dfrac{\mathbf{39}}{\mathbf{14}}$: $\dfrac{2x}{13} = \dfrac{3}{7}$

$2x \times 7 = 3 \times 13$

$14x = 39$

$x = \dfrac{39}{14}$

5. **3**: $\dfrac{3x}{4} - \dfrac{5}{6} = \dfrac{17}{12}$

$\dfrac{3x}{4} \times \dfrac{3}{3} - \dfrac{5}{6} \times \dfrac{2}{2} = \dfrac{17}{12}$

$\dfrac{9x}{12} - \dfrac{10}{12} = \dfrac{17}{12}$

$9x - 10 = 17$

$9x = 27$

$x = 3$

Set 3, Drill 1

1. **2¼**: $\dfrac{9}{4} = \dfrac{8+1}{4} = \dfrac{8}{4} + \dfrac{1}{4} = 2 + \dfrac{1}{4} = 2\tfrac{1}{4}$

2. **4³⁄₇**: $\dfrac{31}{7} = \dfrac{28+3}{7} = \dfrac{28}{7} + \dfrac{3}{7} = 4 + \dfrac{3}{7} = 4\tfrac{3}{7}$

3. **3²⁄₁₅**: $\dfrac{47}{15} = \dfrac{45+2}{15} = \dfrac{45}{15} + \dfrac{2}{15} = 3 + \dfrac{2}{15} = 3\tfrac{2}{15}$

4. **3½**: $\dfrac{70}{20} = \dfrac{60+10}{20} = \dfrac{60}{20} + \dfrac{10}{20} = 3 + \dfrac{10}{20} = 3 + \dfrac{1}{2} = 3\tfrac{1}{2}$

5. **7**: $\dfrac{91}{13} = 7$

Set 3, Drill 2

1. $\dfrac{\mathbf{11}}{\mathbf{3}}$: $3\tfrac{2}{3} = 3 + \dfrac{2}{3} = \dfrac{3 \times 3}{1 \times 3} + \dfrac{2}{3} = \dfrac{9}{3} + \dfrac{2}{3} = \dfrac{11}{3}$

2. $\dfrac{\mathbf{13}}{\mathbf{6}}$: $2\tfrac{1}{6} = 2 + \dfrac{1}{6} = \dfrac{2 \times 6}{1 \times 6} + \dfrac{1}{6} = \dfrac{12}{6} + \dfrac{1}{6} = \dfrac{13}{6}$

3. $\dfrac{\mathbf{45}}{\mathbf{7}}$: $6\tfrac{3}{7} = 6 + \dfrac{3}{7} = \dfrac{6 \times 7}{1 \times 7} + \dfrac{3}{7} = \dfrac{42}{7} + \dfrac{3}{7} = \dfrac{45}{7}$

4. $\dfrac{\mathbf{41}}{\mathbf{9}}$: $4\tfrac{5}{9} = 4 + \dfrac{5}{9} = \dfrac{4 \times 9}{1 \times 9} + \dfrac{5}{9} = \dfrac{36}{9} + \dfrac{5}{9} = \dfrac{41}{9}$

5. $\dfrac{\mathbf{149}}{\mathbf{12}}$: $12\tfrac{5}{12} = 12 + \dfrac{5}{12} = \dfrac{12 \times 12}{1 \times 12} + \dfrac{5}{12} = \dfrac{144}{12} + \dfrac{5}{12} = \dfrac{149}{12}$

Set 4, Drill 1

1. $6.75 \times 10^3 = \mathbf{6,750}$ Move the decimal to the right 3 places.

2. $72.12 \times 10^{-4} = \mathbf{0.007212}$ Move the decimal to the left 4 places

3. $2,346 \times 10^{-3} = \mathbf{2.346}$ Move the decimal to the left 3 places.

4. $27.048 \times 10^2 = \mathbf{2,704.8}$ Move the decimal to the right 2 places.

5. $54.197 / 10^2 = \mathbf{0.54197}$ Because we are dividing by 10^2, we move the decimal to the **left** 2 places.

Set 4, Drill 2

1. $\begin{array}{r} 1.000 \\ + 0.200 \\ + 0.030 \\ + 0.004 \\ \hline 1.234 \end{array}$

2. $\begin{array}{r} 0.\overset{1}{4}8 \\ + 0.02 \\ \hline 0.50 \end{array}$

3. $\begin{array}{r} 1.21 \\ + 0.38 \\ \hline 1.59 \end{array}$

4. $\begin{array}{r} 0.35 \\ - 0.02 \\ \hline 0.33 \end{array}$

5. $\begin{array}{r} 0.\overset{1}{3}70 \\ + 0.042 \\ \hline 0.412 \end{array}$

Set 4, Drill 3

1. **0.54:** $0.27 \times 2 =$
   $27 \times 2 = 54$ Move the decimal to the left 2 places.
   $0.27 \times 2 = 0.54$

2. **1.209:** $0.403 \times 3 =$
   $403 \times 3 = 1{,}209$ Move the decimal to the left 3 places.
   $0.403 \times 3 = 1.209$

3. **0.04:** $0.2 \times 0.2 =$
   $2 \times 2 = 4$ Move the decimal to the left 2 places.
   $0.2 \times 0.2 = 0.04$

4. **17:** $20 \times 0.85 =$
   $20 \times 85 = 1{,}700$ Move the decimal to the left 2 places.
   $20 \times 0.85 = 17$

5. **0.00804:** $0.04 \times 0.201 =$
   $4 \times 201 = 804$ Move the decimal to the left 5 places.
   $0.04 \times 0.201 = 0.00804$

Set 4, Drill 4

1. **0.168:** $2.1 \times 0.08 =$
   $21 \times 8 = 168$ Move the decimal to the left 3 places.
   $2.1 \times 0.08 = 0.168$

2. **0.0252:** $0.063 \times 0.4 =$

    $63 \times 4 = 252$ Move the decimal to the left 4 places.

    $0.063 \times 0.4 = 0.0252$

3. **0.00015:** $0.03 \times 0.005 =$

    $3 \times 5 = 15$ Move the decimal to the left 5 places.

    $0.03 \times 0.005 = 0.00015$

4. **70:** $0.75(80) + 0.50(20) =$ Break this problem into two multiplication problems.

    $0.75 \times 80 = 60$

    $0.50 \times 20 = 10$ Now add the two.

    $60 + 10 = 70$

5. **0.01:** $100 \times 0.01 \times 0.01 =$

    $100 \times 1 \times 1 = 100$ Move the decimal to the left 4 places.

    $100 \times 0.01 \times 0.01 = 0.01$

Set 4, Drill 5

1. **20:** $4/0.2 =$

$$\frac{4}{0.2} \times \frac{10}{10} = \frac{40}{2} = 20$$

2. **42:** $12.6/0.3 =$

$$\frac{12.6}{0.3} \times \frac{10}{10} = \frac{126}{3} = 42$$

3. **80:** $3.20/0.04 =$

$$\frac{3.20}{0.04} \times \frac{100}{100} = \frac{320}{4} = 80$$

4. **7:** $0.49/0.07 =$

$$\frac{0.49}{0.07} \times \frac{100}{100} = \frac{49}{7} = 7$$

5. **12:** $6/0.5 =$

$$\frac{6}{0.5} \times \frac{10}{10} = \frac{60}{5} = 12$$

Set 5, Drill 1

Fraction	Decimal	Percent
1/100	0.01	1%
1/20	0.05	5%
1/10	0.1	10%
1/8	0.125	12.5%
1/5	0.2	20%
1/4	0.25	25%
3/10	0.3	30%
1/3	0.3333…	33.33…%

3/8	0.375	37.5%
2/5	0.40	40%
1/2	0.50	50%
3/5	0.6	60%
2/3	0.6666...	66.66...%
7/10	0.7	70%
3/4	0.75	75%
4/5	0.8	80%
7/8	0.875	87.5%
9/10	0.9	90%
1	1.0	100%

Set 5, Drill 2

1. **0.45:** Convert 45% to a decimal.
   45% becomes 0.45
2. **7/10:** Convert 70% to a fraction.
   70% becomes 70/100, which reduces to 7/10
3. **0.1325:** Convert 13.25% to a decimal.
   13.25% becomes 0.1325
4. **9/25:** Convert 36% to a fraction.

   36% becomes 36/100, which reduces to 9/25

5. **0.0002:** Convert 0.02% to a decimal.

   0.02% becomes 0.0002

Set 5, Drill 3

1. **20%:** Convert 0.20 to a percent.

   0.20 becomes 20%

2. **11/20:** Convert 0.55 to a fraction.

   0.55 becomes 55/100, which reduces to 11/20

3. **30.4%:** Convert 0.304 to a percent.

   0.304 becomes 30.4%

4. **91/200:** Convert 0.455 to a fraction.

   0.455 becomes 455/1000, which reduces to 91/200

5. **3/8:** Convert 0.375 to a fraction.

   0.375 becomes 375/1000, which reduces to 3/8

Set 5, Drill 4

1. 80%: Convert 4/5 to a percent.

   Step 1: $4 \div 5 = 0.8$ $5\overline{)4.0}$ with 0.8 above

   Step 2: 0.8 becomes 80%

2. **50%:** Convert 3/6 to a percent.

Step 1: $3 \div 6 = 0.5$ $6\overline{)3.0}$ with 0.5 above

Step 2: 0.5 becomes 50%

3. **75%:** Convert 9/12 to a percent.

Step 1: $9 \div 12 = 0.75$ $12\overline{)9.00}$ with 0.75 above

Step 2: 0.75 becomes 75%

4. **30%:** Convert 6/20 to a percent.

Step 1: $6 \div 20 = 0.30$ $20\overline{)6.0}$ with 0.3 above

Step 2: 0.30 becomes 30%

5. **150%:** Convert 3/2 to a percent.

Step 1: $3 \div 2 = 1.5$ $2\overline{)3.0}$ with 1.5 above

Step 2: 1.5 becomes 150%

Set 6, Drill 1

1. **120:** Forty percent of the balls in a bag are red. If there is a total of 300 balls in the bag, how many of them are red?

$300 \times 40\% = 300 \times 4/10 = 120$

2. **$40,000:** Sally always puts 15% of her salary in a retirement fund. If she put $6,000 in her retirement fund last year, what was her salary?

Let s = Sally's total salary
$\$6,000 = 15\%$ of s
$\$6,000 = 15/100 \times s$
$\$6,000 = 3/20 \times s$
$\$6,000 \times 20/3 = s$
$\$40,000 = s$

3. **2/5:** Sixteen students wear glasses. If there are forty students total, what fraction of the students wear glasses?

$16/40 = 2/5$

4. **$64:** What is the new price of an eighty–dollar sweater that has been discounted 20%?

If the sweater has been discounted 20%, then the new price is 80% of the original
(because $100\% - 20\% = 80\%$)
$80\% \times \$80 = 4/5 \times \$80 = \$64$

5. **$12.50:** Billy has twenty dollars and Johnny has thirty dollars. If both Billy and Johnny spend 25% of their money on baseball cards, how much money will they invest?

$(0.25 \times \$20) + (0.25 \times \$30) = \$5 + \$7.50 = \$12.50$

Set 6, Drill 2

1. **40%:** Last year, a furniture store sold four hundred chairs, two hundred tables, four hundred couches, and nothing else. The chairs made up what percent of the total items sold?

$400/(400 + 200 + 400) = 400/1000 = 4/10 = 40\%$

2. **$160,000:** At her old job, Sally earned a yearly salary of $80,000. At her new job, Sally earns a salary equal to $40,000 plus a commission of 25% on all her sales. If Sally wants to make a yearly salary at her new job that is the same as that of her old job, how much does she have to produce in terms of yearly sales?

Let s represent the amount of sales that Sally needs to generate in her new job to equal her previous salary.

$\$80,000 = \$40,000 + s \times 25\%$
$\$80,000 = \$40,000 + 1/4\ s$
$\$40,000 = 1/4\ s$
$\$160,000 = s$

3. **60:** Of 250 people surveyed, 36% said they preferred regular soda, 40% said they preferred diet soda, and the rest did not have a preference. How many of the 250 people did not have a preference?

The percent of people who did not have a preference = $100\% - (36\% + 40\%) =$
$100\% - 76\% = 24\%$

The number of people who did not have a preference = $24\% \times 250 =$

$$\frac{24}{100} \times 250 = \frac{6}{25} \times 250 = \frac{6}{\cancel{25}} \times \frac{\cancel{25} \times 10}{1} = 60$$

4. **150:** A jar contains 1/3 red marbles and 1/2 blue marbles. The remaining 25 marbles are white. How many marbles does the jar contain?

First we need to figure out what fraction of the marbles are white. We can do this by figuring out what fraction of the marbles are not white. Add the fractional amounts of red and blue marbles.

$1/3 + 1/2 = 2/6 + 3/6 = 5/6.$

$1 - 5/6 = 1/6$ The white marbles are 1/6 of the total number of marbles.

Let x = total number of marbles.
$25 = 1/6\ x$
$150 = x$

5. **75%:** Ted has 2/3 as many friends as Billy has, and Chris has 1/2 as many friends as Billy has. The number of friends Chris has is what percent of the number of friends Ted has?

Let T = the number of friends Ted has
Let B = the number of friends Billy has
Let C = the number of friends Chris has

$T = 2/3\ B$
$C = 1/2\ B$

$C = x\%\ T\ ?$

$B = 3/2\ T$
$C = 1/2\ (3/2\ T)$
$C = 3/4\ T$
$C = 75\%\ T$

Answer: 75%

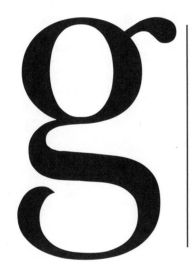

Appendix
of
FRACTIONS, DECIMALS, & PERCENTS

2011 CHANGES TO THE GRE QUANT

In This Chapter . . .

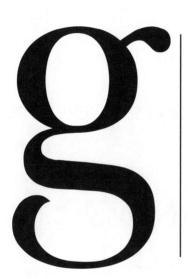

- 2011 Changes to the GRE Quant
- Multiple Choice: Select One or More Answer Choices
- Numeric Entry
- Using the Calculator
- 2011 Format Math Questions

2011 Changes to the GRE Quant

In mid-2011, the Quantitative section of the GRE will undergo a number of changes. Have no fear, however—the actual body of mathematical knowledge being tested won't change, and everything in your Manhattan GRE book(s) will still be relevant and necessary to beat the test. This supplement details everything you need to know to be ready for 2011.

Currently, the GRE contains a single 45-minute quantitative section composed of multiple choice problems, Quantitative Comparisons, and Data Interpretation questions (which are really a subset of multiple choice problems).

After the 2011 changes, test takers will complete two separate 35-minute quantitative sections containing two new problem formats in addition to the current problem formats.

Additionally, a small four-function calculator with a square root will appear on-screen. Truly, many test takers will rejoice at the advent of this calculator! It is true that the GRE calculator will reduce emphasis on computation—but look out for problems in which the order of operations, or tricky wording on percents, is likely to foil those who rely on it too much.

New Problem Formats in Brief:

Multiple Choice: Select One or More Answer Choices – Questions may have from three to seven answer choices, and the test taker is asked to select a certain number of answers ("Which two of the following…") or to select all answers that meet a certain criterion ("Select all that apply").

Numeric Entry – Instead of selecting a multiple-choice answer, test takers type an answer into an entry box, or two entry boxes above and below a fraction bar.

Data Interpretation questions will also occur more often, and the above new problem types will also be used on Data Interpretation; that is, you will be presented with charts or graphs and asked a mix of Multiple Choice: Select One, Multiple Choice: Select One or More, and Numeric Entry questions.

We're about to discuss strategies for each new problem type. But overall, don't worry! The same core mathematical skills are being tested, and any time you've put into studying for the pre-2011 GRE will still be useful for the 2011 GRE. Also, as you're about to see, many of these problem types aren't as different as they might seem.

Finally, don't worry about whether these new problem types are "harder" or "easier." You're being judged against other students, all of whom are in the same boat. So if the new formats are harder, they're harder for other test takers as well. The upcoming strategies and problem sets will put you ahead of the game!

Multiple Choice: Select One or More Answer Choices

The official directions for "Select One or More Answer Choices" read as follows:

Directions: Select one or more answer choices according to the specific question directions.

If the question does not specify how many answer choices to select, select all that apply.

The correct answer may be just one of the choices or as many as all of the choices, depending on the question.

No credit is given unless you select all of the correct choices and no others.

If the question specifies how many answer choices to select, select exactly that number of choices.

Note that there is no "partial credit." If three of six choices are correct and you select two of the three, no credit is given. It will also be important to read the directions carefully.

That said, many of these questions look *very* similar to those you've studied for the "old" GRE. For instance, here is a question that could have appeared on the GRE at any time:

If $ab = |a| \times |b|$, which of the following *must* be true?

    I. $a = b$
    II. $a > 0$ and $b > 0$
    III. $ab > 0$

    A.   II only
    B.   III only
    C.   I and III only
    D.   II and III only
    E.   I, II, and III

Solution: If $ab = |a| \times |b|$, then we know ab is positive, since the right side of the equation must be positive. If ab is positive, however, that doesn't necessarily mean that a and b are each positive; it simply means that they have the same sign.

    I.   It is not true that a must equal b. For instance, a could be 2 and b could be 3.
    II.   It is not true that a and b must each be positive. For instance, a could be −3 and b could be −4.
    III.   True. Since $|a| \times |b|$ must be positive, ab must be positive as well.

The answer is B (III only).

Note that, if you determined that statement I was false, you could eliminate choices C and E before considering the remaining statements. Then, if you were confident that II was also false, you could safely pick answer choice B, III only, without even trying statement III, since "None of the above" isn't an option.

That is, because of the multiple choice answers, it is sometimes not necessary to consider each statement individually. This is the aspect of such problems that will change on the 2011 exam.

Here is the same problem, in 2011 format.

If $ab = |a| \times |b|$, which of the following *must* be true?

Indicate <u>all</u> such statements.

    A. $a = b$
    B. $a > 0$ and $b > 0$
    C. $ab > 0$

Strategy Tip: Make sure to fully "process" the statement in the question (simplify it or list the possible scenarios) before considering the answer choices. This will save you time in the long run!

Here, we would simply select choice C. The only thing that has changed is that we can't do process of elimination; we must always consider each statement individually. On the upside, the problem has become much more straightforward and compact (not every real-life problem has exactly five possible solutions; why should those on the GRE?)

Numeric Entry

The official directions for "Numeric Entry" read as follows:

> Directions: Enter your answer in the answer box(es) below the question.
>
> Equivalent forms of the correct answer, such as 2.5 and 2.50, are all correct. Fractions do not need to be reduced to lowest terms.
>
> Enter the exact answer unless the question asks you to round your answer.

Strategy Tip: Note that you are not required to reduce fractions. It may feel strange to type 9/27 instead of 1/3, but if you're not required to reduce, why take an extra step that has the possibility of introducing a mistake?

In this problem type, you are not able to "work backwards" from answer choices, and in many cases it will be difficult to make a guess. However, the principles being tested are just the same as on the old GRE.

Here is a sample question:

If $x*y = 2xy - (x - y)$, what is the value of 3*4 ?

Solution:

We are given a function involving two variables, x and y, and asked to substitute 3 for x and 4 for y:

$$x*y = 2xy - (x - y)$$

$$3*4 = 2(3)(4) - (3 - 4)$$

$$3*4 = 24 - (-1)$$

$$3*4 = 25$$

The answer is 25.

Thus, you would type 25 into the box.

Using the Calculator

The addition of a small, four-function calculator with a square root means that those taking the 2011 test can forget re-memorizing their times tables or square roots. However, the calculator is not a cure-all; in many problems, the difficulty is in figuring out what numbers to put into the calculator in the first place. In some cases, using a calculator will actually be less helpful than doing the problem some other way.

On the new 2011 GRE, you will be provided with a simple on-screen calculator. For this practice set, you may use any calculator, but don't use any functions other than $+$, $-$, $\times$, $\div$, and $\sqrt{}$.

> If x is the remainder when (11)(7) is divided by 4 and y is the remainder when (14)(6) is divided by 13, what is the value of $x + y$?

Solution: This problem is designed so that the calculator won't tell the whole story. Certainly the calculator will tell us that $11 \times 7 = 77$. When you divide 77 by 4, however, the calculator yields an answer of 19.25. The remainder is *not* 0.25 (a remainder is always a whole number).

You might just go back to your pencil and paper, and find the largest multiple of 4 that is less than 77. Since 4 DOES go into 76, we can conclude that 4 would leave a remainder of 1 when dividing into 77. (Notice that we don't even need to know how many times 4 goes into 76, just that it goes in. One way to mentally "jump" to 76 is to say, *4 goes into 40, so it goes into 80... that's a bit too big, so take away 4 to get 76*).

However, it is also possible to use the calculator to find a remainder. Divide 77 by 4 to get 19.25. Thus, 4 goes into 77 nineteen times, with a remainder left over. Now use your calculator to multiply 19 (JUST 19, not 19.25) by 4. You will get 76. The remainder is $77 - 76 = 1$. Therefore, $x = 1$.

Use the same technique to find y. Multiply 14×6 to get 84. Divide 84 by 13 to get 6.46... Ignore everything after the decimal, and just multiply 6 by 13 to get 78. The remainder is therefore $84 - 78 = 6$. Therefore, $y = 6$.

Since we are looking for $x + y$ and $1 + 6 = 7$, the answer is 7.

2011 Format Fractions, Decimals, & Percents Questions

On the new 2011 GRE, you will be provided with a simple on-screen calculator. For this practice set, you may use any calculator, but don't use any functions other than $+$, $-$, $\times$, $\div$, and $\sqrt{}$.

1. $\dfrac{\dfrac{3}{4} - 0.72}{\dfrac{6}{25}}$ is equal to which TWO the following?

   A. 8

   B. $\dfrac{1}{8}$

   C. 0.125

   D. 12.5

   E. $\dfrac{25}{2}$

   F. $\dfrac{16}{2}$

2. If x is 35% of y, then y is what fraction of x?

3. If Mr. Smart invested between $40 and $100, inclusive, and at the end of the investment period, found that his investment was worth between $110 and $120, inclusive, which of the following COULD be the percent increase of the value of his investment?

   Indicate <u>all</u> such statements.

   A. 20%
   B. 75%
   C. 175%
   D. 240%

4. What is $\dfrac{2{,}700 \times 10^{7}}{0.0003 \times 10^{10}}$ written as an integer?

1. Note that the answer choices form pairs: A is equal to F, B is equal to C, and D is equal to E. So one of these pairs must be the answer.

Calculator solution: Use the calculator to subtract $\frac{3}{4} - 0.72 = 0.03$. DO NOT type $0.03 \div \frac{6}{25}$ into the calculator. This will generate a PEMDAS error and an incorrect answer. Instead, type in $\frac{6}{25}$ to get 0.24.

Now type in $0.03 \div 0.24$ to get 0.125. If you didn't know that $\frac{1}{8} = 0.125$, you would have to type the fractional answers into the calculator as well to see which choice is equal to 0.125 (since you were told that exactly two choices are correct).

Does that seem like it creates too much potential for error? Remember, the calculator is not a cure-all. Here is a non-calculator solution.

When simplifying decimals mixed with fractions, remember that *decimals are easier for adding and subtracting and fractions are easier for multiplying and dividing.*

$$\frac{\frac{3}{4} - 0.72}{\frac{6}{25}} = \frac{0.75 - 0.72}{\frac{6}{25}} = \frac{0.03}{\frac{6}{25}} = \frac{\frac{3}{100}}{\frac{6}{25}}$$

Remember that dividing by a fraction is the same as multiplying by the reciprocal:

$$\frac{3}{100} \times \frac{25}{6} = \frac{1}{8}$$

The answer is B and C.

2. The calculator is probably not helpful here. Write "x is 35% of y" as math and simplify:

$$x = \left(\frac{35}{100}\right) y$$
$$x = \frac{7y}{20}$$

Now solve for y:

$$y = \frac{20x}{7} \text{ OR } y = \frac{20}{7} x$$

The answer is $\frac{20}{7}$.

3. Let's calculate the maximum and minimum return Mr. Smart could have made. Any choices that fall within that range are valid.

To get the minimum return, start Mr. Smart off with the largest amount and have him end with the smallest amount. If he began with $100 and ended with $110, his investment went up by 10%.

To get the maximum return, start Mr. Smart off with the smallest amount and have him end with the largest amount. If he began with $40 and ended with $120, his money tripled. That's a 200% increase (because we have double the amount ON TOP OF the original amount, and "double" = 200%). Or, use the percent change formula (and feel free to use the calculator):

$$\text{Percent Change} = \frac{80}{40} \times 100 = 200\%$$

Any values between or including 10% and 200% are valid.

The answer is A, B, and C.

4. There are many ways to simplify here, but one good way is to turn 2,700 and 0.0003 into 27 and 3 by manipulating the powers of 10. This will allow us to divide 27 by 3 to get 9, and then we'll see how many zeroes we have left.

Remember, *when dealing with powers of 10, when a number gets bigger, its exponent gets smaller, and vice-versa.* Thus, $2,700 \times 10^7 = 27 \times 10^9$ (we made 2,700 smaller by two decimal places, so we had to make the power of 10 get bigger by two decimal places to compensate).

Similarly, $0.0003 \times 10^{10} = 3 \times 10^6$ (we made 0.0003 larger by four decimal places, so the power of 10 gets smaller by four decimal places). Thus:

$$\frac{2,700 \times 10^7}{0.0003 \times 10^{10}} = \frac{27 \times 10^9}{3 \times 10^6}$$

It might be helpful to split into two fractions:

$$\frac{27}{3} \times \frac{10^9}{10^6} = 9 \times 10^3 = 9,000$$

Alternately, you could try a calculator solution, but you would need to convert to integers before plugging in to the calculator, since you don't have access to exponents on the calculator. So you would have to type $27,000,000,000 \div 3,000,000$. Most people will make a mistake doing this, so we recommend the non-calculator solution above.

The answer is 9,000.

Finally, a GMAT® prep guide series that goes beyond the basics.